Especially for

....

From

....

Date

....

Print ISBN 978-1-63058-732-1
Special Edition ISBN 978-1-63409-304-0

eBook Editions:
Adobe Digital Edition (.epub) 978-1-63409-241-8
Kindle and MobiPocket Edition (.prc) 978-1-63409-242-5

Published by Barbour Books, an imprint of Barbour Publishing, Inc., P.O. Box 719, Uhrichsville, Ohio 44683, www.barbourbooks.com

Our mission is to publish and distribute inspirational products offering exceptional value and biblical encouragement to the masses.

Member of the
Evangelical Christian
Publishers Association

Printed in China.

God, Grant Me

Serenity

Devotional Prayers
for Mothers

Renae Brumbaugh

BARBOUR BOOKS
An Imprint of Barbour Publishing, Inc.

*To Charis and Foster,
two of my greatest blessings.
Through you, God has given me
the desires of my heart.*

*And to God, whose goodness
far exceeds my ability to describe it.
To You be the glory and
honor forever. I love You.*

Contents

Introduction

I forgot to set the alarm. But somehow, I managed to get everyone dressed and out the door with ten seconds to spare, each with a plastic cup of chocolate milk and a slice of bread with peanut butter—breakfast of champions.

That's when the darling boy child tripped and sloshed his milk all down the front of his clean clothes and into the interior of my newly vacuumed car. He stood there looking at me, eyes wide, milk running down his chin, dripping from his T-shirt, streaming down his jeans and into his sneakers. In that moment, I had a decision to make.

Many such moments have happened in the course of my motherhood career. I wish I could say I've always made the right choices, but I haven't. Far too many times I've allowed frustration to spew all over the pallete of my family's emotional portrait, leaving ugly, hurtful stains. I wish I could rewind those moments and choose a different path, but I can't. All I can do is try to make different, better choices moving forward.

I'm so glad we serve a forgiving God. I'm also glad He had the foresight to make children forgiving creatures. When we bathe our mistakes in lots of kisses and with "I'm sorry" and "I love you," our children bounce back pretty well.

The prayers in this book are my attempt at choosing tranquility, peace, and the higher path when life lowballs me. I invite you to join me on this journey as together we draw near to our God . . . the source of our serenity.

In Your Presence

Honor and majesty are [found] in his presence;
strength and joy are [found] in his sanctuary.
1 Chronicles 16:27 AMP

Dear Father, many days I wonder where I'll find the strength to go another step. I'm weary and worn out, and my joy is zapped. On those days, it's good to know where I can find strength and joy: in Your presence. It's true. . .when I make time in my busy schedule to spend quality time with You, I feel restored. I feel peace. I even feel a strength and majesty from knowing I'm a child of the King. Lord, I don't know why I forget to spend time with You when there are so many benefits. Other demands close in. There are chores to be done, mouths to feed, boo-boos to kiss. Remind me, Lord, in the midst of the madness, to carve out time to renew my spirit. I need to daily replenish the strength and joy I know can only be found in You. Amen.

Finding Rest

*And he said, "My presence will go with you,
and I will give you rest."*
EXODUS 33:14 ESV

Dear Father, how did You know how tired I get? I guess it's further proof that You do know me better than anyone, that You never leave me, and that You care about me. I'm humbled and amazed at the thought of You following me through my day simply because You love me and want to spend time with me. I'm awed by the idea that You are closer than the beat of my heart, and no matter what happens, You're right there to give me wisdom and comfort. When I remember I'm not alone—that You walk each step with me—it calms my spirit. It makes me feel rested and renewed, even when my body is exhausted. Thank You for going with me, Lord. Thank You for giving me rest. Amen.

Doting Grandfather

You will make known to me the path of life;
In your presence is fullness of joy;
In your right hand there are pleasures forever.
PSALM 16:11 NASB

Dear Father, there are so many times I don't know which way to go, which decision to make, or which direction to choose. Thank You for this reminder that if I stay close to You, You'll show me which path leads to life and rest, peace and joy. When I remain in Your presence, You lead the way. I don't have to follow a roadmap if I follow You. And that's not the only benefit of staying near You, Lord. Like a doting grandfather, You keep special treats in Your pocket. In Your presence I'll find joy and everlasting pleasure. What great motivations for staying close to You! Thank You, Lord, for all the good things I find in Your presence. Amen.

Secret Place

*You hide them in the secret place of Your presence
from the conspiracies of man; You keep them
secretly in a shelter from the strife of tongues.*
PSALM 31:20 NASB

Dear Father, the little childhood rhyme that says, "Sticks and stones may break my bones, but words will never hurt me," isn't true. You know words can hurt much more than physical blows. Father, I take precautions to protect myself physically: I wear a seatbelt, I look before I cross a busy street, and I avoid dangerous situations. But protecting my heart from people's words is much more difficult. Words fly out of nowhere and find the weakest place in my armor. They stab my heart, and the pain lasts. Father, thank You for this beautiful reminder that You'll hide me away in Your presence. When I stay close to You, You keep my heart and my emotions in a safe place. Hide me in Your secret place today, Lord. Amen.

Refreshing Presence

Therefore repent and return, that your sins may
be wiped away, in order that times of refreshing
may come from the presence of the Lord.
ACTS 3:19 NASB

Dear Father, I repent. I am a sinner, and I'm sorry for the things I've done that have hurt You and others. Please forgive me, Lord. I don't want to be that way or do those things anymore. Thank You for Jesus, who took the punishment for my sins so I could have a right relationship with You. Father, I don't want my sin to keep me from spending time in Your presence, but I know You can't be in the presence of my sin. Wash me, Lord, and make me clean and pure. More than anything, I want to be with You. I long to hold You, sit in Your lap, and rest. Thank You for refreshing me with Your presence. Amen.

Joyful Singing

---

*Serve the L*ORD *with gladness;*
Come before Him with joyful singing.
PSALM 100:2 NASB

Dear Father, do You ever get tired of hearing about my worries and woes and complaints? I know You're always glad to listen to me, but I get tired of hearing other people complain, if that's all they do. I wonder if You ever feel that way about my complaints. Lord, I'm sorry if I forget to sing and laugh and be cheerful in Your presence. I'm sorry if I serve You with a heavy heart when You've given me so much to be happy about! Today, I want to serve You with gladness and carry a song of praise deep in my spirit. When I start to worry and fret and feel anxious, remind me of Your goodness and all I have to be thankful for. I want to come before You with joyful singing. Amen.

Giving Thanks

Surely the righteous will give thanks to Your name;
The upright will dwell in Your presence.
PSALM 140:13 NASB

Dear Father, thank You for so many things. Thank You for my
family. Sometimes I get so caught up in taking care of them,
I forget to be grateful for them. But I know each member of
my family is a beautiful gift from You, and I'm so thankful that
You let me be in their lives. Thank You for taking care of us by
providing the food we need, comfortable shelter, and money
to pay the necessary bills. Father, I have so many things to be
thankful for, but the thing I'm most grateful for is Your presence.
Thank You for allowing me to spend time with You. Thank You
for staying close and for walking with me through my days.
I know that even when I feel alone, I'm not, for You've promised
to never leave me. Amen.

Pure Spirit

Create in me a clean heart, O God, and renew a steadfast spirit within me. Do not cast me away from Your presence, and do not take Your Holy Spirit from me.
PSALM 51:10–11 NKJV

Dear Father, I truly want to please You. I want to have a clean heart and a pure spirit, for I know these qualities bring You pleasure. I know I fall short, but I also know You look at our hearts, our desires, and our motivations. I truly long to make You happy. When impure thoughts and ambitions sneak in, send Your Holy Spirit to gently guide me back on course. I want my thoughts, words, and actions to bring You pleasure, Lord. I want my life to be a delight to You. Please don't cast me away from Your presence, and if there's anything in my life that gets in the way of my relationship with You, remove it. I love You, Father, and I love living my life close to You. Amen.

Nowhere to Run

Where can I go from Your Spirit?
Or where can I flee from Your presence?
PSALM 139:7 NKJV

Dear Father, sometimes I feel alone. I know You promised to never leave me, but sometimes it feels like You're not around at all. I call out to You, but I don't hear Your voice. I reach for You, but I can't feel Your presence. That's when I have to fall back on my faith. I know You honor Your Word. I know You keep Your promises. So I know You're with me even when I can't feel You. I know You hear me, even when I can't hear You. Even if I try to run from You, I can never outrun Your love. If I try to hide from You, there's no place You don't see. Thank You for sending Your Spirit with me everywhere I go. I know You are there every minute, every breath. I trust You. Amen.

In Love

But for me it is good to be near God;
I have made the Lord GOD my refuge,
that I may tell of all Your works.
PSALM 73:28 ESV

Dear Father, I love being near You. I wish I had the words to describe how much I love spending time with You. It's kind of like that feeling of first being in love, when I just can't wait to see the person, when I think about them all the time, when I'm overcome by the simple brush of their hand. That's how I feel about You, Lord. I'm head over heels in love with You, and I love being in Your presence. Father, You are my safe place, my refuge. Like a child who buries her face in her father's neck, I long to bury myself in Your mighty arms. From the safety of Your grip, I want to tell the world how much I love You and how great You are. Thank You for keeping me close, Father. Amen.

Peace, Be Still

*And he arose, and rebuked the wind, and said
unto the sea, Peace, be still. And the wind ceased,
and there was a great calm.*
MARK 4:39 KJV

Dear Father, You are amazing. You command the wind and
the sea. You call order from chaos. I know if You control
the forces of nature, You can calm my anxious spirit.
When my children are fussy and whiny, call forth peace
into my soul. When the spaghetti boils over and I can't
find my phone and I feel like everybody wants more from
me than I can give, help me hear Your hushed whisper:
Peace, be still. I need the calm that only You can give,
and my children need the security that comes from a
serene mother. Let Your tranquility spill over into their lives
as You help me make our home into a safe harbor. Amen.

Wits' End

They reeled and staggered like drunkards; they were at their wits' end. Then they cried out to the LORD in their trouble, and he brought them out of their distress. He stilled the storm to a whisper; the waves of the sea were hushed.
PSALM 107:27-29 NIV

Dear Father, I know what it's like to be frustrated. Every day, it seems like I arrive at my wits' end at some point or another. Being a mother is the hardest job I've ever had, with the life of another person totally dependent on my care. At times, it feels like I'll explode with the pressure. But Lord, being a mother is also the most rewarding job I've known. Those moments of sweet snuggles or landmark events send the other, more stressful times into the shadows. When I'm in the middle of chaos, help me take refuge in the sweetness of motherhood. When I cry out to You, still me with the hushed lullaby of Your love. Amen.

Controlled by Peace

*You were chosen to live together in peace.
So let the peace that comes from Christ
control your thoughts. And be grateful.*
COLOSSIANS 3:15 CEV

Dear Father, thank You for calling me to live a peaceful life. I
know that's what I've been created to do. I want Your peace to
be the driving force in my life, but it seems the forces of chaos
want to steer me in another direction. I know one way to find
peace is to be thankful for all the good things in my life. Thank
You for my family, for my children, for my job. Thank You for
loving me and giving me people to love. Thank You for the many
blessings I often overlook. Help me to notice the little things
as well as the bigger blessings in my life. I want Your peace to
control my heart and to guide every aspect of my life. Amen.

Seek Peace

Turn from evil and do good;
seek peace and pursue it.
PSALM 34:14 NIV

Dear Father, I want to turn from evil, in any form. Whether it's impatience or angry thoughts or the television shows I watch or the music I listen to, help me reject anything that isn't from You. I also want to do the good that you've placed me here to do. Many of the noble deeds You require of me are deeds that will go unnoticed by everyone except You, but help me do them anyway. Remind me to find joy in the small tasks that bless others, whether they notice or not. Finally, help me to pursue peace in the face of chaos. I want to make a habit of responding in peace, no matter what comes my way. When my children look at me, I want them to feel the calm assurance of Your love. Amen.

Be Still

*Be still before the Lord
and wait patiently for him.*
PSALM 37:7 NIV

Dear Father, this verse reminds me to be still and wait for You.
Be still? I can barely remember a time when *still* was a part of
my vocabulary. Yet I know when chaos swirls around me, You
will bring a stillness to my spirit, if I let You. That's hard, Lord.
It's hard not to become absorbed in the tightly packed schedule
of soccer games and ballet lessons, and the phone ringing
and the doorbell buzzing. It's hard not to focus completely on
my hungry family and the dirty toilets and the pressing emails
and text messages. Help me today, Lord, to silence my phone,
turn off my television, and do whatever it takes to be still in
You. Bring me to that place of quietude, if not in my outer
circumstances, then in the inner spaces of my heart. Amen.

Perfect Peace

*You will keep in perfect peace those whose
minds are steadfast, because they trust in you.*
ISAIAH 26:3 NIV

Dear Father, I want to live in perfect peace. You promised
You'd keep us in a place of tranquility, as long as we keep an
unwavering focus on You. I want to dedicate my entire life to
You, Lord. My words, my thoughts, my actions. . .they're all
Yours. My money, my time, and my commitments are all Yours.
Every part of my life I commit to You. I want my mind to remain
steadfastly centered on You, on Your love, and on Your desires
for me. I trust You with my dreams, my ambitions, and my goals.
I trust You with my family and my finances. Every concern I
have, I leave in Your hands. Thank You for loving me, and for
promising perfect, unwavering peace. Amen.

Recipe for Peace

Justice will produce lasting peace and security.
ISAIAH **32:17** CEV

Dear Father, thank You for giving me the recipe for peace. Sometimes I use all the wrong ingredients but hope for a calm, serene lifestyle anyway. Instead of showing patience, I respond in anger. Instead of acting in kindness, I offer harshness. When I should show compassion and love, I give in to the stress and blow my fuse. Some days, I'm just too tired to behave righteously. But Lord, I know You have provided all the components for serenity. All I have to do is take them, mix them into my life, and allow their delicious scents to waft through my circumstances and into the lives of those I love. Help me today, Father, to read the recipe carefully and choose the ingredients of patience, kindness, and love. Amen.

Blessed Are the Peacemakers

Blessed are the peacemakers,
for they will be called children of God.
MATTHEW 5:9 NIV

Dear Father, I want to be a peacemaker. When all is still, it's easy to stand by my resolution to pursue peace no matter what. But when the storms threaten and the chaos ensues, my resolve gets lost in the din. Anxiety and tension take over, and before I know it, I'm adding to the turmoil instead of extinguishing it. I need Your help, Lord. I know that no matter what happens around me, Your peace is available to me. After all, peace comes from within, from that place of connection from my heart to Yours. I want to bring Your peace into my home, my job, my family. I want to repay harshness with kindness, envy with generosity, and indifference with love. Remind me in those moments of turmoil to be a peacemaker. Amen.

Free Gift

*I give you peace, the kind of peace that only
I can give. It isn't like the peace that this world
can give. So don't be worried or afraid.*
JOHN 14:27 CEV

Dear Father, thank You for giving me Your peace. It's a gift
You've offered freely to Your children. It's not something I have
to work for or earn . . . it's mine. All I have to do is take it. But I
can't hold onto my troubles and Your peace at the same time.
It's an awkward juggling act, and the troubles always take
over, crashing to the floor around me and leaving me in chaos.
In order to have Your gift of peace, I must lay down my fears,
lay down my worries and concerns, and leave them at Your feet.
Then I have room in my arms—in my heart and life—for the calm
serenity You've given me. Thank You, Lord. Amen.

Hearing the Whisper

*I have told you this, so that you might have peace
in your hearts because of me. While you are in the world,
you will have to suffer. But cheer up!
I have defeated the world.*
JOHN 16:33 CEV

Dear Father, thank You for this reminder. When distress fills my world, when chaos swirls around me, it's not necessarily my fault. It's just part of living in this world. But You have conquered this world! You've gained the victory over my anxiety and my circumstances. And since You live in me, that means victory over all things is mine, as well. As long as I trust You in all circumstances, I'll have peace. But Lord, that's easier said than done, for the turmoil always screams right in my ear while Your peace is more of a gentle whisper. Help me to have serenity in the midst of pandemonium. Help me to listen closely and hear Your hushed voice. Amen.

Lay It Down

*Come to me, all you who are weary
and burdened, and I will give you rest.*
MATTHEW 11:28 NIV

Dear Father, sometimes I feel so weary, so weighted down with responsibilities and worries, I don't know if I can take another step. But then I remember, I'm not supposed to shoulder all of that. You're standing right there—each moment—arms open wide, offering to carry my load. All I have to do is hand it over to You, then follow You while You cart all my concerns in Your all-consuming love. You love me, and You'll take care of everything. Oh, I know I still have to be responsible. But as long as I'm doing my best and staying close to You, You'll take care of me. I can walk around free as a bird if I'll just trust You with my troubles. Remind me to do that today, Lord. I love You. Amen.

Trust Him

Trust in the Lord with all your heart, and do not lean on your own understanding. In all your ways acknowledge him, and he will make straight your paths.
PROVERBS 3:5–6 ESV

Dear Father, why do I try so hard to figure things out by myself? I strive and worry, and I try to manipulate circumstances so everything will turn out exactly as I think they should. But things don't always go according to plan, Lord. I often don't understand why things turn out as they do, but I trust You. I know that as long as I stay close to You, as long as I look to You before I act, You will work things out according to plan—*Your* plan. I know the path You'll lead me on will be much straighter and much smoother than if I try to navigate on my own. Help me remember today, Lord, to trust You, to look to You, and to follow You. Amen.

Lay It Down

Let all bitterness and wrath and anger and clamor and slander be put away from you, along with all malice. Be kind to one another, tenderhearted, forgiving one another, as God in Christ forgave you.
EPHESIANS 4:31–32 ESV

Dear Father, I know I'm not supposed to hold on to anger, bitterness, and hurt. I'm not supposed to slander and gossip about others, even if they've injured me. But sometimes, when pain is etched so deeply, it helps to talk about it. I want to nurse my wound; I long to open it up and examine it. But Lord, I know You're the one who brings healing. You're the one I should talk to about my emotional pain, rather than talking to others. By continually pulling apart the incision, I actually prolong the pain and delay the healing. Lord, help me to lay my hurts and wounds at Your feet, and leave them there. Help me to forgive, to love again, and to move forward with the peace-filled life You have for me. Amen.

Talk About It

Do not be anxious about anything, but in everything by prayer and supplication with thanksgiving let your requests be made known to God. And the peace of God, which surpasses all understanding, will guard your hearts and your minds in Christ Jesus.
PHILIPPIANS 4:6–7 ESV

Dear Father, I'm so glad You gave Your permission for me to ask for exactly what I want. I don't have to worry that I'm being petty or selfish; if I am being that way, You'll let me know. You just want me to talk to You. In Your great wisdom, You know that the act of talking about my problems, my dreams, and my desires will help bring peace to my heart. You created us for relationships, and relationships are built through time spent talking. Father, one thing I want is serenity, and I know You want that for me as well. Thanks for listening, Lord, and thank You for Your peace. Amen.

Puzzle Pieces

And we know that for those who love God
all things work together for good,
for those who are called according to his purpose.
ROMANS 8:28 ESV

Dear Father, I love You. I love You with my whole heart, with all that is in me. More than anything, I want to live out Your purpose for my life. I want each day to be another puzzle piece, filling in the plan You had from the beginning. I know that as long as I remain focused on my love for You and on fulfilling Your purpose for me, I don't have to worry about how the pieces fit. You'll work it all out in time, and when You do, it will be a work of art. Remind me, Lord, when I feel anxious about my life and my future, that You've got it all under control. You love me, and You have good things in store for me. Amen.

Humble Yourself

Therefore humble yourselves under the mighty hand of God, that He may exalt you at the proper time, casting all your anxiety on Him because He cares for you.
1 Peter 5:6–7 NASB

Dear Father, I don't like to humble myself. It's hard. After all, I think my ideas are best. My plans are surely the most sensible ones. And when things don't go according to my design, I balk. But Lord, when I hang on to my ideas, when I get upset that things don't go the way I want them to, I'm really saying that my game plan is superior to yours. Father, help me to be humble enough to realize that I'm tiny, and You are enormous. While many things are impossible for me, all things are possible with You. Help me to lay my plans, cares, and anxieties at Your feet and trust in Your perfect love for me. Amen.

Peace and Holiness

*Make every effort to live in peace with everyone
and to be holy; without holiness
no one will see the Lord.*
HEBREWS 12:14 NIV

Dear Father, I know I should try to live at peace with those around me. Sometimes it's hard when they don't make the effort to be peaceful. But Lord, I must confess, it's not always them. Too often I'm the one who speaks harshly, who stirs up trouble and refuses to forgive. Help me to be a peacemaker even when others don't show the same effort. Help me to lay down my feelings of anger and hurt as I do everything in my power to live peacefully with everyone. I know You've called me to be different, to live a life set apart from the way most people act. You've called me to be holy, and holiness is an important factor in achieving a serene, peaceful life. Thank You for helping me today and every day. Amen.

Like Them

Therefore, since we have so great a cloud of witnesses surrounding us, let us also lay aside every encumbrance and the sin which so easily entangles us, and let us run with endurance the race that is set before us, fixing our eyes on Jesus, the author and perfecter of faith.
HEBREWS 12:1–2 NASB

Dear Father, thank You for the stories of great men and women of faith who let go of everything and believed You'd take care of them. I want to be like them, Lord. I want to "run with endurance" the way they did. It's easy to admire their faith without imitating it. But I don't want to just be an admirer. I want to be included in Your list of people who really trusted You. I can only imagine the peace that would be mine if I really let go of it all, knowing You are in control and that You have a beautiful plan for my life. Help me to make that kind of faith a reality, Lord. Amen.

Just Like You

Let all bitterness and wrath and anger and clamor and slander be put away from you, along with all malice. Be kind to one another, tender-hearted, forgiving each other, just as God in Christ also has forgiven you.
EPHESIANS 4:31–32 NASB

Dear Father, I want to live a life of serenity. Unfortunately, I want to hang on to things that upset me, and that's not conducive to the peace-filled life I long for. When people irritate me or hurt me, I don't want to lay that down. I don't want to forgive. I want to hold on to it and make them pay, or make sure they're aware of what they did to annoy me. When I see it in writing like this, it sounds so mean. Father, You've been so gracious to forgive me of the numerous things I've done to hurt You. You've shown infinite patience. Help me to be kind, as You are kind. Help me to be tender-hearted and forgiving, just like You. Amen.

Keep Quiet

A fool gives full vent to his spirit,
but a wise man quietly holds it back.
PROVERBS 29:11 ESV

Dear Father, I don't want to think what would happen if You weren't so patient with me. You have many reasons to chew me up and spit me out and to tell me exactly what You think of my sin and my foolish mistakes. But You don't do that. You deal gently with me. Most of the time, You speak in whispers instead of shouts. Often You remain quiet, loving me into repentance instead of demanding it. Why can't I treat others that way? I want to be a mirror of Your love, Lord. When I'm frustrated, help me to lay down my annoyance and remain quiet. I want to invite others into a calm, peaceful relationship. Harsh words and irritation will only build walls and drive wedges. Help me to always respond in serenity and love. Amen.

No Answers

I will instruct you and teach you in the way you should go; I will counsel you with my eye upon you.
PSALM 32:8 ESV

Dear Father, I really need Your instruction and counsel. I wish I could talk to You face to face and hear Your voice. I have so many questions I'd like You to answer. Father, I know all of life's answers are addressed in Your Word, but some situations aren't addressed directly, and there are times when I don't know what to do. Even when I seek You and comb through Your Word, there are no clear answers for some of my issues. Father, in times like these, please stay close to me. I don't want to make bad choices or wrong decisions, but I don't know what the right choices are. I guess that's when I just have to do the best I can and trust You with the outcome. Stay near me, Father. Teach me, guide me, and counsel me. I need Your help. Amen.

Counselors

Where there is no guidance, a people falls,
but in an abundance of counselors there is safety.
Proverbs 11:14 esv

Dear Father, thank You for giving such good advice, such
wisdom in Your Word. You didn't just leave me with a book to
read; You gave me Your Holy Spirit. Beyond that, You taught me
how to maintain a system of checks and balances in my life so
I can feel confident in my decisions. After I seek You and read
Your Word, after I pray about something and do my best to
make a good decision, sometimes I'm still not sure. You told me
to seek wise counselors. The more I talk to people about what
I'm going through, the more warnings or confirmations I receive.
I know I must be careful to seek the advice of wise people;
it won't do me any good to seek out fools who may only tell me
what I want to hear. Help me to humble myself and seek wise
counsel when I need it. Amen.

Place of Honor

*But sanctify the Lord God in your hearts, and always
be ready to give a defense to everyone who asks you a
reason for the hope that is in you, with meekness and fear.*
1 PETER 3:15 NKJV

Dear Father, I want to sanctify You in my heart. I want to give
You such a special place of honor that people will notice You
whenever they see me. Father, what a wonderful thought—
to have to defend the hope that radiates from my life because of
Your presence! That's what I want to happen, Lord. I want people
to ask me why I have such joy and peace, such serenity and
hope. When they do, I want to point them to You. Sometimes,
I lose track of the hope I have in You. When my serenity gets lost
in a pile of rotten circumstances, remind me to set You back on
the throne of my life. Amen.

Wide Road

There is a way which seems right to a man,
but its end is the way of death.

PROVERBS 14:12 NASB

Dear Father, it's hard living in a day and age where sinful behavior is viewed as normal and righteousness is mocked. It's difficult being the object of ridicule in the media because of my belief in Your Word. Father, help me to stand firm in my decision to serve You, and help me stay calm, meek, and peaceful in the way I deal with those who oppose Your ways. It's easy to make a few adjustments in my thinking here and there so my views fit in better with the people around me. But I don't want to adjust my views if it means compromising Your principles. Help me to avoid destructive paths in my own life, and help me to lead others to You. Amen.

According to Your Faith

Then he touched their eyes, saying,
"According to your faith be it done to you."
MATTHEW 9:29 ESV

Dear Father, is it really done to me according to my faith? Is that really how it works? Because honestly, some days my faith feels pretty weak. I know You are good. I know You are mighty and powerful. But when it comes to trusting You with the details of my life, I have a hard time. I know that faith—total and complete trust in Your care—is a decision I must make every single day. Too often, I want to take the rudder and steer my own boat so I'll know where it's going. Help me to trust in Your goodness, Your kindness, and Your mercy. Remind me that when I let go and trust You, I may not always know the destination, but I know it will be someplace good. Amen.

Decisions, Decisions

Multitudes, multitudes, in the valley of decision!
For the day of the LORD is near in the valley of decision.
JOEL 3:14 ESV

Dear Father, every single day, I journey through the valley of decision. Will I show patience, or not? Will I remain calm, or not? Will I trust You, or not? My days are filled with mundane moments that have life-shaping potential. When will I learn that it's not the big stuff that alters the course of our lives? It's the little decisions, day by day and minute by minute, that carve out the paths of our lives. Lord, all too often I make the wrong choices. I snap. I respond harshly instead of with kindness. I allow the wrong things to absorb my time, instead of pouring my life into loving those around me. Help me today as I'm faced with opportunities to make those little decisions that add up to so much . . . help me to choose wisely. Amen.

Misplaced Keys

*I will give you the keys of the kingdom of heaven,
and whatever you bind on earth shall be bound
in heaven, and whatever you loose on earth
shall be loosed in heaven.*
MATTHEW 16:19 ESV

Dear Father, You know how forgetful I am. I'm always losing my keys. I get distracted and set them down somewhere, and then I forget where I put them. But those keys hold power; without them, I can't start my car or get into the places I need. Just as my car keys hold power, You've given me the power of the kingdom of heaven. And just as I misplace my car keys, I often forget to use the power You've given me. When chaos presents itself and I want to explode from the stress, I have power to respond in peace. I have power over my circumstances, not the other way around. Today and every day, help me to remember to use Your keys. Amen.

Martha, Martha

But the Lord answered her, "Martha, Martha, you are anxious and troubled about many things, but one thing is necessary. Mary has chosen the good portion, which will not be taken away from her."
LUKE 10:41-42 ESV

Dear Father, thank You for the story of Mary and Martha. I think I have a little of both of those ladies in me. At times, I get so anxious and stressed. I have a schedule and an agenda, and I just want to get things done. And honestly, the people in my life don't always get that. It's important to be like Martha . . . without her, many tasks would go undone. But Mary knew how to let a few things go in favor of a more important goal. She knew relationships always take precedent over work. Sometimes, it's best to take a deep breath, leave the chores, and bask in the presence of those we love. Help me be a Martha when it's needed; help me be a Mary when it counts. Amen.

Life and Peace

My son, do not forget my teaching, but let your heart keep my commandments, for length of days and years of life and peace they will add to you.
PROVERBS 3:1–2 ESV

Dear Father, thank You for Your Word. I know the things You say are full of wisdom and life. When I follow Your commands, my circumstances may not be perfect. But consistently obeying Your statutes leads me, step by step, toward the peaceful life I so desire. Serenity doesn't come in one great swoop, but in inches, in tablespoonsful of good choices. Lord, help me to live daily by Your Word. Help me to model it for my children and teach it to them. I want them to have full, happy, peaceful lives, too. Today, as I make all those little choices, hold my hand. Whisper Your Word in my ear, and remind me to choose life and peace. Amen.

Follow Me

Then Jesus told his disciples, "If anyone would come after me, let him deny himself and take up his cross and follow me. For whoever would save his life will lose it, but whoever loses his life for my sake will find it."
MATTHEW 16:24-25 ESV

Dear Father, many of my decisions are based on making life easier for myself, not harder. But You said to deny myself. You said to take up my cross—my heavy burden—and follow You. I know You don't want me to deny myself just for the sake of denial. Rather, You want me to put others first. You want me to make hard choices to show love to others. You want me to postpone immediate pleasure in order to save up for greater reward down the road. Father, help me to deny myself in favor of others today. Help me to lay down my life for those I love. I know by doing so, I'll find a greater peace than I ever thought possible. Amen.

Soul Song

*And Mary said: "My soul glorifies the Lord
and my spirit rejoices in God my Savior."*
LUKE 1:46–47 NIV

Dear Father, I love the way Mary's spirit rejoiced in You. Her soul glorifies You. Deep in the most secret places of her thoughts, she magnified You. I want to be like that, Lord. I want You to so completely fill my life that even when I'm not thinking about You, I sense Your presence. Even when I'm focused on the mundane tasks of being a mother, of being an adult, I want my spirit to sing You a song of praise. Father, I know that kind of commitment doesn't happen overnight. Rather, it's born of a lifetime of decisions to honor You and focus on You and love You. I want to be so enamored with You that my soul basks in Your presence, even when my mind is elsewhere. Amen.

Top Priority

But seek first his kingdom and his righteousness,
and all these things will be given to you as well.
MATTHEW 6:33 NIV

Dear Father, every now and then, it's good for me to step back and take a look at my routines. What am I seeking? In what am I investing my time, energy, money, and resources? When I look at how I spend my time, I must admit, I spend a lot of energy on good things. But all too often I leave out the best thing. It's good to want my family to have nice things. It's good to do my best to take care of them by working hard, doing the laundry, cooking, and cleaning. . .but if those things take top priority in my life, I've got things out of order. Remind me today and every day to seek You first. I know that as long as I'm giving You top priority, You'll take care of the rest. Amen.

Pretty Words

He replied, "Isaiah was right when he prophesied about you hypocrites; as it is written: These people honor me with their lips, but their hearts are far from me."
MARK 7:6 NIV

Dear Father, what a harsh thing to say! Isaiah called the people hypocrites, even though they made a habit of worshiping You. Their words honored You, but their hearts didn't. They sang pretty hymns of praise and quoted lofty platitudes, but they lived pretty much the way they wanted to live. Their empty words had little impact on their spirits. Lord, I don't want to be like that. I don't want to be a hypocrite. I want every part of my life to be a living praise song to You. I want my heart to stay as close to You as it can possibly get. Help me make my thoughts and my actions match the words I sing at church. Amen.

Routine Worry

Do not let your hearts be troubled.
You believe in God; believe also in me.
JOHN 14:1 NIV

Dear Father, I feel troubled about many things. When You work one problem out, another shows up to take its place. Sometimes, I think worry has become such a routine for me, that I'm not sure how to function without it. What do I do when a troubled heart has become a habit? I've heard the best way to undo a bad habit is to replace it with a better one. Help me to replace my fear and anxiety with trust. Remind me, Lord, when trials come, to remember who You are and what You can do. Instead of stressing about things, I want to make faith a normal everyday practice. I want to develop a pattern of trust in my life. I know that's the only way to truly experience the peace You want me to have. Amen.

The Great Pursuit

Pursue love, and desire spiritual gifts.
1 CORINTHIANS 14:1 NKJV

Dear Father, it seems like all day long I'm chasing something or somebody. I'm chasing down the dirty laundry, or I'm chasing my kids from one rehearsal or sports league to the next. But while I'm chasing all these things, I need to make sure I'm chasing love with my whole heart. I want to pursue those qualities You desire for my life. It's interesting that the very things that will challenge my patience, kindness, and serenity are the things that give me opportunities to strengthen those virtues. When my children are messy, it's an opportunity to practice patience. When they drive me crazy with the same repetitive requests, it's a chance to exercise kindness and love. Father, remind me to pursue Your gifts, for I know they hold the keys to lasting peace in my life. Amen.

Total Makeover

*Do not be conformed to this world, but be
transformed by the renewal of your mind,
that by testing you may discern what is the will
of God, what is good and acceptable and perfect.*
ROMANS 12:2 ESV

Dear Father, I need a makeover. I'm not talking about an all-
expense-paid shopping spree with new hair, clothes, and
makeup, though that would be nice. Lord, my spirit needs a
makeover. My mind needs to be renewed, and my soul needs to
be transformed. My thought patterns often mirror the thought
patterns of the world I live in, instead of Your thoughts. My
actions resemble the world's actions, instead of what You'd have
me do. Lord, I want my life to be good and acceptable in Your
eyes. Remind me to consistently spend time in Your Word and in
prayer, as I try to remodel my mind in Your image. Amen.

Hard Work

*In all things I have shown you that by working hard
in this way we must help the weak and remember
the words of the Lord Jesus, how he himself said,
"It is more blessed to give than to receive."*
ACTS 20:35 ESV

Dear Father, thank You for this reminder to work hard. I know that true blessings don't flow from looking out for myself or from expecting others to do things for me. The real blessing is gained when I pour myself out for others. Oh, it may be frustrating at times. I may get tired. But when I spend my life loving other people, the payoff comes by their love for me. It comes by having long-term, positive, abundant relationships with those people. When I empty myself into the lives of others, You fill me with a joy that can't be replaced. Teach me this concept, and help me make habits of working hard and giving to others. Amen.

Highest Form of Flattery

Therefore be imitators of God, as beloved children.
EPHESIANS 5:1 ESV

Dear Father, they say imitation is the highest form of flattery. I've noticed my children imitating me—from the way I walk and talk to the way I take care of my home and family. I love it when people say they look like me, but it's sobering to hear people say they act like me. It hurts when they do something undesirable and I realize they learned it from me. Father, the only way I can help them develop good, virtuous qualities in their lives is to live out those qualities in front of them. If I imitate You, and they imitate me, they'll ultimately be acquiring the building blocks of godly character. Father, just as my children adore me and want to be like me, I adore You. I want to be just like You as much as possible. Help me to keep my eyes on You, so I can look like You in every situation. Amen.

Old Habits

No temptation has overtaken you that is not common to man. God is faithful, and he will not let you be tempted beyond your ability, but with the temptation he will also provide the way of escape, that you may be able to endure it.
1 CORINTHIANS 10:13 ESV

Dear Father, You know better than I do about those habits in my life that need to be eliminated. Whether it's the words I say, the way I respond to stress, or the way I spend my time, habits are hard to break. Although I want to overcome these habits, temptation always strikes at my weakest moments. Yet, You promised You'd be there to help me. In my own strength, I may not make much progress, but with Your strength, I can do anything. Help me today, Lord, to draw on Your power when I feel powerless. Help me to eliminate bad habits and replace them with qualities that will please You and help me love others better. Amen.

Standing Guard

My son, be attentive to my words; incline your ear to my sayings. Let them not escape from your sight; keep them within your heart. For they are life to those who find them, and healing to all their flesh. Keep your heart with all vigilance, for from it flow the springs of life.
PROVERBS 4:20-23 ESV

Dear Father, help me to guard my heart. It's easy to get distracted and let my guard down, and before I know it, unholy words, thoughts, and images flood my mind and assault my senses. I need to be vigilant in my watch, for in many ways, my thoughts set the tone for my household. If I feel angry, my family feels defensive. If I feel unsettled, so do they. Help me to surround myself with calm, positive, uplifting messages. Remind me to block anything from my home that doesn't reflect Your goodness and love. Help me to guard my heart, Father, for in doing so, I'm also protecting my family. Amen.

Think About These Things

Finally, brothers, whatever is true, whatever is honorable, whatever is just, whatever is pure, whatever is lovely, whatever is commendable, if there is any excellence, if there is anything worthy of praise, think about these things.

PHILIPPIANS 4:8 ESV

Dear Father, I've heard it's human nature to focus on the negative. But Lord, when I gave my life to You, You gave me access to a new heart and a new way of thinking. Help me reprogram my mind to think the way You think. Instead of becoming angry at lies, I can focus on the beauty of Your truth. Instead of setting my mind on dishonorable, unjust events, I can set my thoughts on the honorable and the just. I can reflect on the loveliness of my child's face or the simple beauty in a field of flowers. And if I run out of noble things on which to meditate, I can always turn my full attention to You. Remind me today and every day to think about these things. Amen.

Choose Joy

A joyful heart is good medicine,
but a crushed spirit dries up the bones.
PROVERBS 17:22 ESV

Dear Father, sometimes my spirit feels crushed. And when I feel that way, it's hard to focus on anything else. I just want things in my life to be right and good and healthy, and when they're not, it affects every part of me. Father, I may not have power over my circumstances, but I can control my thoughts. Help me to set my mind on things that bring me joy and happiness. I want to set my mind on things like Your love and all the beautiful gifts You've given me. Even if it's just a tiny speck of sunlight in a dark room, help me focus on the light. I know the practice of meditating on joy instead of gloom will heal both my body and my spirit, and my joyful spirit can help heal others, as well. Remind me today, Lord, to choose joy. Amen.

Mind-set

Set your mind on the things above, not on the things that are on earth. For you have died and your life is hidden with Christ in God.
COLOSSIANS 3:2–3 NASB

Dear Father, so many things grab my attention. It's like a great contest, with this object and that event competing for my thoughts. I want to fill my mind with heavenly reflections, but it's hard to focus when so many circumstances clamor to occupy space. But Lord, my brain space is valuable real estate. Why would I use it to store items with little or no value? Surely, I'd be better off keeping beautiful, noble thoughts there. I want to set my mind on things above. Lord, I love the idea that my life is hidden in You. Help me to hide my thoughts in You as well. Protect my mind from those things that don't increase Your love. Amen.

Heart, Soul, and Mind

*And He said to him, "You shall love the Lord
your God with all your heart, and with
all your soul, and with all your mind."*
MATTHEW 22:37 NASB

Dear Father, I love this verse. It is truly my desire to love You
with all my heart, soul, and mind. That's a noble thought, but
my desires don't always equal my reality. My thoughts can turn
from pure to polluted before I know it. My mind can be wholly
focused on You, and out of nowhere, something happens—
somebody says or does something—and my sweet meditations
are poisoned with anger, resentment, or jealousy. All I know to
do, Lord, is to stand under the flow of Your love and forgiveness,
and let my relationship with Your Son purify my thoughts again
and again. As imperfect as I am, Lord, here I am. I love You. I'm
Yours: heart, soul, and mind. Amen.

Teach Me to Love

*The one who does not love does
not know God, for God is love.*
1 John 4:8 NASB

Dear Father, help me to love. It seems the longer I live, the more
I realize that I don't have this love thing mastered yet. I love You,
but I don't always show it through my actions. I love my children,
but sometimes I get impatient with them. I love my family and
friends, but sometimes I act selfishly. Lord, I want to love like
You love. I know that's my highest calling and the reason You
placed me here—so I could love other people. I don't want to fail
at this calling, Lord. I want to know You more and more; for the
more I know Your character, the easier it will be to imitate You.
Teach me to love so well that when people are around me, they'll
know they've been touched by You. Amen.

Number My Days

*So teach us to number our days, that we
may present to You a heart of wisdom.*
PSALM 90:12 NASB

Dear Father, I know life is short, but sometimes it seems so
long. Some days I get so tired and worn out, and it feels like
this season will go on forever. But as long as some hours may
seem, I know they'll fly by, adding together and vanishing like
a mist. I'll wake up one morning and my children will be grown.
They'll move away and begin their own lives, and I'll miss them.
I'll long for those little moments that seem to drag now. Teach
me to make the most of every moment. Instruct me to guard
my thoughts against things that will steal my minutes, my days,
and my years. I want to honor You and love well each moment of
my life. Amen.

Here and Now

I would have despaired unless I had believed that
I would see the goodness of the Lord
in the land of the living.
PSALM 27:13 NASB

Dear Father, I know You are good. I know that You have beautiful plans for my life—plans for joy, happiness, and love. Yet I sometimes find myself submitting to feelings of despair, as if I don't believe in Your goodness. Why do I do that, Lord? I can look back on my life thus far and see You've never failed me. You've always come through with kindness, compassion, and generosity. Remind me who You are, Lord. When I give in to anxiety about today and fear of tomorrow, remind me that I will see Your goodness—right here on earth, right now in this life. I don't have to wait for heaven to experience the good things You have in store. Thank You for Your goodness, Lord. I trust You. Amen.

Knowing You

How precious also are Your thoughts to me, O God!
How vast is the sum of them!
PSALM 139:17 NASB

Dear Father, I want to know You. Every day, I want to learn more about Your personality and Your character. But You are so deep and Your thoughts are so vast, I know I can never even scratch the surface. Lord, You said we are to imitate You. The best way to impersonate You is to study You, memorize You, and learn about all the facets of Your being. Father, You truly are precious to me. Like an exquisite treasure, I want to study You from every angle, admiring every feature. I want to know Your thoughts and understand Your ways so I can be more like You. I want my thoughts to be Your thoughts and my ways to be Your ways. Let me know You today, Lord. Let me see You. Amen.

Search Me

Search me, O God, and know my heart; Try me and know my anxious thoughts; and see if there be any hurtful way in me, and lead me in the everlasting way.
PSALM 139:23–24 NASB

Dear Father, I really want to make this verse my prayer, but when You search my heart, it's kind of like performing surgery. It hurts! When You shine Your light on my soul, I know You'll find all sorts of potentially dangerous things. Like precancerous cells, those sinful thoughts need to be removed. If left alone, they'll grow, fester, and take over my life. Eventually, they'll destroy me and hurt those around me. Search me, Lord. Use Your great spotlight to magnify those things in my life that need to be removed. Using Your Word as a knife, cut away the parts that are harmful, and leave only the portions of my life that will allow me to glorify You and love others. I trust You, and I love You. Amen.

Watching My Steps

The steps of a man are established by
the LORD, and He delights in his way.
PSALM 37:23 NASB

Dear Father, I want my steps to be established by You. I know You give me a free choice, and I can choose to walk my own path if I desire. But Lord, when I follow my own roadmap, I always end up lost, in the middle of nowhere, out of gas, and with no cell phone reception. At least that's the way it feels. When I allow You to determine my course, I don't always understand where You're taking me. But I trust You and know You'll never lead me to a place of harm. Father, I want You to be happy with my steps and delight in my way. I know that only happens when I follow You. Help me to walk in Your shadow, Lord, and to step ahead only when I'm sure it's the way You want me to go. Amen.

The Love of Money

---

*Make sure that your character is free from
the love of money, being content with what
you have; for He Himself has said, "I will never
desert you, nor will I ever forsake you."*
HEBREWS 13:5 NASB

Dear Father, I tell myself I don't love money. Yet, I often find myself longing for a bigger house, a nicer car, or snazzier clothes. I envy my friends who are able to send their children to private school or take big vacations. Lord, You've blessed me with so much. Help me be content with what I have. Give me a greater understanding that the true riches in life cannot be attained with money. Help me to spend my time wisely, investing in relationships and developing my ability to love. I know that no matter what I *think* I want, I have all I need in You. Thank You for Your constant presence in my life. Amen.

Root of Evil

For the love of money is a root of all kinds of evils.
It is through this craving that some have wandered away
from the faith and pierced themselves with many pangs.
1 TIMOTHY 6:10 ESV

Dear Father, everywhere there are advertisements designed
to pique my interest and make me want a certain product. It's
a subtle brainwashing, and if I'm not careful, I'll succumb to it.
Whether it's for a new purse or a new car, Lord, I want to spend
my money carefully. I want my money to be used to help people
and to show love. Sometimes the appropriate way to spend
money is on a new outfit so I can make my husband proud he
married me. Sometimes the new outfit can wait and that money
can be used to feed a homeless person or buy a child a new
coat. Help me to look at money the way You do, as a resource of
Your love. Amen.

Whom Do I Serve?

No one can serve two masters, for either he will hate the one and love the other, or he will be devoted to the one and despise the other. You cannot serve God and money.
MATTHEW 6:24 ESV

Dear Father, I want to serve You and You alone, but it's really hard not to feel like a servant—or even a slave—to money. Bills must be paid. Groceries must be bought. And in order for my children to take part in many of the activities that make childhood fun, we need money. It's a fact of life, and the need for money isn't going away. Please give me a wise perspective on money. Teach me to view it as a tool to accomplish Your work rather than a goal in itself. Remind me each day about what's important. I want to serve You with everything I have, and that includes my money. Amen.

Only Trust Him

"Therefore do not be anxious, saying, 'What shall we eat?' or 'What shall we drink?' or 'What shall we wear?' For the Gentiles seek after all these things, and your heavenly Father knows that you need them all."
MATTHEW 6:31-32 ESV

Dear Father, I trust You. I don't know why I worry about money sometimes. I guess I'm just human, and I like to know ahead of time that I have the money I need to provide for my family. Life happens—cars break down, emergencies occur, and sometimes, we have extra expenses we didn't plan for. That's when I worry the most, Lord, but I know from Your Word and from experience that You will take care of me. You know about life's unplanned events long before I do, and I know You'll provide for every need. Help me not to be anxious, but trust only in You. Amen.

Top Priority

But seek first the kingdom of God and his righteousness,
and all these things will be added to you.
MATTHEW 6:33 ESV

Dear Father, sometimes I think I'm seeking You, but I'm not really seeking You first. Other things get in the way. They fill my thoughts and demand my attention: I seek to calm the babies or have coffee with my friends or clean my house or find money in the budget for that big vacation. Lord, many of these are good things, but if I allow them to squeeze in front of my relationship with You, they're wrong. Show me how to prioritize my life so You stay at the top of my list and everything else falls beneath. After all, when You come first, I'll love better. I'll be a better mother, friend, and employee. And I've found that when I'm putting You first, You find extra special ways to bless me and those I love. Remind me to seek You first, today and every day. Amen.

What Dreams Are Made Of

*He who loves money will not be satisfied
with money, now he who loves wealth
with his income; this is also vanity.*
ECCLESIASTES 5:10 ESV

Dear Father, it's fun to think about what I'll do someday when
I have the money to do it. I imagine a bigger, more beautiful
home. I dream of expensive vacations on the beach, with
assistants bringing me cool lemonade. I picture a luxury car with
all the bells and whistles. But Lord, I know people who have
those things, and they still have problems. Many of those people
aren't satisfied with what they have. I'm the same way. I have
so much more than many people of the world. It's humbling to
remember that the very things I've already been blessed with
are the stuff someone else dreams of. Help me to be satisfied
with what I have. Teach me to recognize and enjoy the blessings
in my life today. Amen.

Wise Investment

*Do not lay up for yourselves treasures on earth,
where moth and rust destroy and where thieves break
in and steal, but lay up for yourselves treasures in
heaven, where neither moth nor rust destroys and
where thieves do not break in and steal. For where
your treasure is, there your heart will be also.*
MATTHEW 6:19–21 ESV

Dear Father, I confess. I have a savings account, I plan for my retirement, and I put things back for a rainy day. I don't think this verse is telling me not to do these things. I think the caution comes in knowing that despite our plans, life happens and plans fail. If all my hope lies in my retirement plan or my savings account, I'll be disappointed. But when I spend my life investing in others—investing in becoming the person You created me to be and pouring out Your love to the people You've placed in my life—I'll see a limitless return on that investment. Help me to invest wisely today, Lord. Amen.

Spending and Saving

*Precious treasure and oil are in a wise man's
dwelling, but a foolish man devours it.*
PROVERBS 21:20 ESV

Dear Father, I like to buy stuff. It's fun to go shopping for new things, even if that shopping is done on the Internet. As a matter of fact, it's easier now than ever to spend money without ever leaving my home. But Lord, if I'm not careful, I can spend an entire paycheck on this and that before I know it. If I consistently waste money on things my family doesn't really need, I'm no different than the fool who devours his treasure and oil. Give me wisdom in my spending. I don't want to be a tightwad nor do I want to be careless with my money. Help me know when to spend and when to save, so my family can always have what they need. Amen.

Eye of the Needle

*Again I tell you, it is easier for a camel to go
through the eye of a needle than for a rich
person to enter the kingdom of heaven.*
MATTHEW 19:24 ESV

Dear Father, I've been told that the eye of the needle was a
gate leading into Jerusalem. It was small, and poor people
who traveled on foot could get through easily. But the
wealthy, who typically travelled with camels loaded with
goods, had a harder time. They had to unload their camels,
carry their packages through on foot, then come back and
get their camels to kneel. The camels had to scoot through on
their knees. It was hard, but not impossible, for the wealthy to
get through that gate. Remind me of this verse when I want to
acquire things I don't need. Those things may seem desirable,
but often, they'll just make it harder for me to reach my goal
of becoming like You. Amen.

Poured Out

*Bring the full tithe into the storehouse, that there
may be food in my house. And thereby put me to
the test, says the L*ORD *of hosts, if I will not open
the windows of heaven for you and pour down
for you a blessing until there is no more need.*
MALACHI 3:10 ESV

Dear Father, I know I can't outgive You, but it sure is fun to try.
Not that I'm giving to get back from You—I just know that's part
of the equation. When I give my time or money to You, You open
up my schedule and resources and give back to me. When I give
love to other people, the love that's returned is immeasurable.
Remind me of this when I'm feeling spent, like I don't have anything to give. I want to give to please You. And I want to open
myself up for Your blessings poured out onto me. Amen.

Whatever You Ask

*Therefore I tell you, whatever you ask in prayer,
believe that you have received it, and it will be yours.*
MARK 11:24 ESV

Dear Father, what a great promise this is! Did you really mean *anything*? Anything at all? I guess one of the things I need to remember is that when I'm talking to You every day, my desires conform to Your desires for me. When I'm walking with You, the things I ask for will be things You want me to have. Even if they're not, it's okay to ask. You'll either grant my request or conform my desires. That's a win-win situation. Lord, I can think of times when I've asked for something You've not given. Even so, I trust You. I trust Your desire to make me happy. I like to give good things to my children, and I know You're a much more loving parent than I will ever be. Remind me to have faith in Your goodness and in Your love for me. Amen.

A Righteous Person

*The prayer of a righteous person
is powerful and effective.*
JAMES 5:16 NIV

Dear Father, thank You for the assurance that the prayers
of the righteous hold weight with You. I guess the question
I must ask myself is, am I a righteous person? I want to be.
More than anything, I long to please You. I know a righteous
person is humble, forgiving, compassionate, patient,
and virtuous. I want to be all those things, Lord, but I know
I fall short. I'm so grateful that You look at our hearts, for there
You can see I'm really trying. Little by little, with Your help,
I'm becoming righteous. Because of that, I know I can come to
You with anything, and You will carefully consider my requests.
It feels pretty special to know my words hold power with You.
Thank You, Father. I love You. Amen.

What Pleases Him

And whatever we ask we receive from him,
because we keep his commandments
and do what pleases him.
1 JOHN 3:22 ESV

Dear Father, this Scripture amazes me. It takes my breath away to think that when we live to please You, You'll give us what we ask for. I know You'll never give me something that will harm me or lead me down the wrong path; You love me too much for that. But when I live in a close relationship with You, when I walk closely with You every day, my desires naturally conform to Your will for my life. Lord, I want more than anything to please You. I want my life to be a beautiful song that brings a smile to Your face. I want my words, thoughts, and actions to bring joy to Your heart. I love You with all that I am. Thank You for loving me, too. Amen.

Your Will

*And this is the confidence that we have toward him,
that if we ask anything according to his will he hears us.
And if we know that he hears us in whatever we ask, we know
that we have the requests that we have asked of him.*
1 JOHN 5:14–15 ESV

Dear Father, I know if I ask something that's in Your will, You'll do it. So how do I know Your will? I keep forgetting that You're not trying to hide Your plan from me. If I'm spending time with You every day, reading Your Word, trying to live according to Your laws, confessing my sins, and trying really hard not to do them again, I'm in Your will. You want me to obey You. You want me to share Your love with others. You want me—and my family—to live happy, peaceful lives. Thank You for the confidence that You'll give me what I ask for when I ask according to Your will. Amen.

Abide in Me

If you abide in me, and my words abide in you,
ask whatever you wish, and it will
be done for you.
JOHN 15:7 ESV

Dear Father, I want to abide in You. You likened "abiding" to the branches of a vine. You are the vine itself, and as long as the branches are joined to the vine, they will remain strong and healthy. But when they become detached, they lose connection with the life source, and they die. Father, I want to remain attached to You, and I know prayer is the key to that attachment. I want to stay close to You, drawing my very life from Your words. I want my thoughts, words, and actions to flow from the fuel of Your love. Help me to keep a constant connection with You as we share each day in sweet conversation. Thank You for Your promises, Father. I love You. Amen.

Any Time

Pray without ceasing.
1 THESSALONIANS 5:17 ESV

Dear Father, sometimes I feel lonely. Even in the midst of the chaos which is my life, I long for someone to talk to . . . someone who understands. Yet, I don't have to long for that kind of companionship. I have You, and You have promised never to leave me or forsake me. I love talking to You through my thoughts and silent prayers during the day. I love sharing secrets with You as together we laugh over something my children did or ponder some new truth. No matter where I am or what I'm doing, You're there to listen and even respond. Thank You for sharing that never-ending conversation with me. I draw strength and wisdom from our talks, and from the knowledge that I can start and stop a conversation with You at any time because You're always there. I love You, Father. Amen.

Great and Hidden Things

*Call to me and I will answer you, and will tell you
great and hidden things that you have not known.*
JEREMIAH 33:3 ESV

Dear Father, often when I pray, I do all the talking. I call to
You and I know You listen, and that's a great comfort to me.
But sometimes I forget that in order for us to have a true
conversation, I need to let You talk, as well. Sometimes You
speak to me through Your Word, as Your Holy Spirit reveals
things to me that I've not understood before. Other times, I can
hear Your whisper in my heart, and I know You're telling me
things I need to know. Your words—both the written ones and
the whispers—are important guide posts on my life's journey.
Speak to me today, Father. Answer my questions and tell me
great and hidden things I've never before understood. I love You,
and I'm glad I have You to guide me. Amen.

Teach Us to Pray

Now Jesus was praying in a certain place, and when he finished, one of his disciples said to him, "Lord, teach us to pray, as John taught his disciples."

LUKE 11:1 ESV

Dear Father, teach me to pray. I know prayer is just a conversation with You. But when I converse with others, I don't like it if the other person does all the talking. I don't care for conversations where my thoughts, words, and ideas aren't valued. Sometimes when I talk to You, I've noticed I do most of the talking. Father, I love You, and I value Your wisdom. You are beyond my comprehension, too wonderful for words. Forgive me for being self-centered. I'd much rather be You-centered. Help me to teach my children to pray as You teach me to pray. Thank You for taking the time to converse with me, Father. I love You. Amen.

If We Confess

*If we confess our sins, he is faithful and just to forgive us
our sins and to cleanse us from all unrighteousness.*
1 JOHN 1:9 ESV

Dear Father, I am a sinner. There's no hiding that fact. And when
I mess up in a big way, I'm often the first to admit it. I fall on my
knees before You and ask for Your forgiveness and for healing
of the mess I've created. But Lord, it's often those little sins—like
gossip or mild rebellion—that keep me down and hinder my
communication with You. I wink at the little sins, because, after
all, they're not *that* bad. Father, I don't want anything to stand in
the way of my relationship with You. Open my eyes, and help me
recognize everything in my life that doesn't measure up to Your
standard. I confess my sins and my sinfulness. Thank You for
Your forgiveness, cleansing, and healing in my life. Amen.

Blessings

Bless the LORD, O my soul, and all that is within me,
bless his holy name! Bless the LORD, O my soul,
and forget not all his benefits, who forgives all your
iniquity, who heals all your diseases, who redeems
your life from the pit, who crowns you with steadfast
love and mercy, who satisfies you with good so that
your youth is renewed like the eagle's.
PSALM 103:1–5 ESV

Dear Father, one meaning of the word *bless* is to speak good things about someone. Even with all the words in every language ever written, I'd never be able to fully describe Your goodness. I want to bless You every moment of the day as my spirit remembers all Your beautiful qualities. Thank You for Your forgiveness. Thank You for Your healing power over my body and my emotions. Thank You for pulling me out of bad situations and placing me in better, safer places. I want to wear Your love like a crown so everyone can see Your influence in my life. Amen.

The Proper Time

A time to love, and a time to hate;
a time for war, and a time for peace.
ECCLESIASTES 3:8 ESV

Dear Father, thank You for the reminder that there really is an appropriate time for everything. Sometimes I get so caught up in my own goals and my own agenda that I forget there is a time to set my schedule aside and just relax, or just be present in the moment. When my children need me, help me to pay attention. When You offer a beautiful sunset or a field of flowers, remind me to take time to appreciate them. And when it is time to work, help me to be a diligent worker. Show me each moment, Father, the best way to use that time. I don't want to waste my hours. Teach me to use them wisely as I observe the proper time for each thing You allow me to do. Amen.

In Your Hands

My times are in your hand; rescue me from the hand of my enemies and from my persecutors!
PSALM 31:15 ESV

Dear Father, my times really are in Your hands. At least, I want them to be. I don't want to be in charge of my schedule, because when that happens, I often accomplish the less important things and miss out on the really great opportunities. Rescue me, Father, from enemies that will steal my time. Rescue me from unimportant phone calls, from television shows that distract me from my children, from social media that robs me of face-to-face relationships. Rescue me from thoughts that keep me from being present with my family. Save me from things that sneak into my schedule and swallow my hours, leaving nothing to show for them. I give my moments, hours, and days to You, Father. Show me how to spend them wisely. My times are in Your hands. Amen.

Firstfruits

*Honor the LORD with your wealth and
with the firstfruits of all your produce.*
PROVERBS 3:9 ESV

Dear Father, what does it mean to honor You with the firstfruits of my produce? If I were a farmer, it would mean I give you the first—the best—of what my farm produces. If I translate that into every area of my life, that means whatever I do, I give You the first and *the best*. When I make my schedule, I schedule You first. I don't try to squeeze You into what's left over. It means I spend quality time with You at whatever time of day I'm at my best. When I do that, You infuse me with energy, power, and strength for the rest of my day. You infuse me with peace and serenity so I can face whatever may come with dignity, grace, and joy. I want to give You the firstfruits of my schedule, Lord. Amen.

Wise Use of Time

*Look carefully then how you walk, not as unwise
but as wise, making the best use of the time,
because the days are evil. Therefore do not be foolish,
but understand what the will of the Lord is.*
EPHESIANS 5:15–17 ESV

Dear Father, I want to be wise with my time. I'm easily distracted with many people and things competing for my attention. In the moment, they all seem worthy and important. Sometimes it's not until much later that I realize which things were valuable and which were a waste of time. Help me to see with Your eyes, Father. Direct my days, and remind me to always choose people over things. Repeat to my spirit as often as needed that my family is more important than television or social media. At the end of my life, I want my family's recollections to be filled with beautiful memories of love and laughter. Help me to invest my time loving and building relationships before there's no time left to do that. Amen.

Big Plans

Come now, you who say, "Today or tomorrow we will go into such and such a town and spend a year there and trade and make a profit"—yet you do not know what tomorrow will bring.
JAMES 4:13–14 ESV

Dear Father, I love to plan things. I love to dream about tomorrow and what may happen with this or that. I know You have good things in store for my life, and I like to think about and hope for the future. But it's easy to get so caught up in planning for the future that I forget what's important today. I work to put money away for retirement, but I won't enjoy my retirement years if my relationship with my children is strained. Help me to focus on today, on this moment, on building up the people You've placed in my life, on loving them and nurturing those relationships. Remind me, Father, that I have no promise of an earthly tomorrow. What I do with today has eternal value. Amen.

Remind Me

O Lord, make me know my end and what is the measure of my days; let me know how fleeting I am! Behold, you have made my days a few handbreadths, and my lifetime is as nothing before you. Surely all mankind stands as a mere breath!
Psalm 39:4-5 esv

Dear Father, remind me that life is short. Remind me that I will take a breath and my children will be grown with families of their own. Help me to use my hours wisely and invest my time in eternal things. Sometimes, no matter how good my plans or how honorable my intentions may be, my life doesn't go according to schedule. When things interrupt my plans, help me respond with patience. Help me keep a smile on my face and a song in my heart. Give me serenity in my day, no matter what happens, as I model Your love for the people around me. Amen.

God's Schedule

But do not overlook this one fact, beloved, that with the Lord one day is as a thousand years, and a thousand years as one day. The Lord is not slow to fulfill his promise as some count slowness, but is patient toward you.
2 PETER 3:8-9 ESV

Dear Father, thank You for this reminder that my agenda isn't Your agenda. You have Your own schedule, and Your timing is perfect. I'm not the most patient person in the world, Lord. When I decide I want something, I want it right now. I want that new furniture now. I want my loved one to be healed of cancer right now. I want relationships to be mended right now. I don't want to have to wait for things, Lord. But more often than not, it's in the waiting time that valuable lessons are learned, and my spirit makes real progress in its journey toward becoming like You. Teach me patience and help me trust in Your schedule. Amen.

While There's Time

*We must work the works of him who sent me while
it is day; night is coming, when no one can work.*
JOHN 9:4 ESV

Dear Father, why do I procrastinate when it comes to making
memories? Why do I put off playing with my children—talking
to them and creating radiant recollections for their memory
banks—for stuff that has no eternal value? I forget how
important it is to be present with my children, how vital it is
that I love them with the gift of my time. It seems like they'll be
young forever and there will always be another opportunity to
make a memory, but I know that's not true. Help me to build
beautiful memories with my family today, right now in this
moment. Help me remember that now is the time to live out my
purpose, which is to love. Help me love now while there's still
time. Amen.

Doing My Job

He said to them, "It is not for you to know times or
seasons that the Father has fixed by his own authority.
But you will receive power when the Holy Spirit has come
upon you, and you will be my witnesses in Jerusalem and
in all Judea and Samaria, and to the end of the earth."
ACTS 1:7–8 ESV

Dear Father, sometimes I try to do Your job, and I forget to
do mine. Scheduling the events of this life is Your job. I can
trust You and Your perfect timing. I don't need to worry about
tomorrow or what the future holds—that's all in Your capable
hands. My job is to do what You've called me to do: share Your
love with everyone I can. Remind me to do my job today, Lord.
Teach me how to do it better and more effectively. I want to love
people with all that I am today. I trust You with tomorrow. Amen.

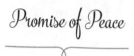

Promise of Peace

My son, do not forget my teaching, but let your heart keep my commandments, for length of days and years of life and peace they will add to you.
PROVERBS 3:1–2 ESV

Dear Father, the three things You promise here are things I want more of in my life. I want longer days—I never have enough time to do everything I need. I want to live a long time—not sickly in a nursing home but healthy, toting my children's children around and making beautiful memories for as long as I have breath. Finally, I want peace. After all, what good is a long life if it's filled with stress and hardship? Thank You for this formula for longer days, longer life, and peace. I know if I remember Your words and my heart beats in obedience to You, You'll bless me with these things. I do want to please You every day of my life. Amen.

Faith Meets Action

What good is it, my brothers, if someone says he has faith but does not have works? Can that faith save him? If a brother or sister is poorly clothed and lacking in daily food, and one of you says to them, "Go in peace, be warmed and filled," without giving them the things needed for the body, what good is that? So also faith by itself, if it does not have works, is dead.
JAMES 2:14–17 ESV

Dear Father, when someone is hurting or in need, You rely on my willingness to take care of them. I want my actions to match the faith I say I have. I especially want them to match when it comes to my family, Lord. When I'm at home, it's easy to take off my best face and let stress rule my actions, but Father, I want my actions to be a living, breathing example of Your love for them. Help my actions to match my faith today and every day. Amen.

When Faith Meets Action

But someone will say, "You have faith and I have works."
Show me your faith apart from your works, and I will
show you my faith by my works.
JAMES 2:18 ESV

Dear Father, anybody can do good works. Anybody can donate their money to some foreign cause or their time to a soup kitchen. So what sets Your children apart? What makes my faith any better than someone who doesn't believe in You, but does good things in the world? I know the difference is You. When I work with all I have to make a difference in this life, You send Your Holy Spirit to fill in the gaps. When faith meets action, miracles happen. When faith meets action, mountains are moved and lives are changed. My faith, added to my diligent effort, calls on Your power. Thank You for infusing my actions with Your presence, Lord. Amen.

Whatever I Do

Whatever you do, work heartily, as for the Lord and not for men, knowing that from the Lord you will receive the inheritance as your reward. You are serving the Lord Christ.
Colossians 3:23–24 esv

Dear Father, teach me what it means to work heartily. It's easy to look for shortcuts and for opportunities to leave my work unfinished to take advantage of a more pleasant task. Sometimes I work hard, but I grumble about the work I do. I know You want me to put forth a vigorous effort with a song in my heart! You want me to pour my energy and my heart into the duties You've placed before me whether it's in employment that brings a paycheck or my jobs at home. I know that whatever I do, I'm representing You. Whatever I do, I do for You. I want to serve You heartily, Lord. Amen.

Rich in Good Works

They are to do good, to be rich in good works,
to be generous and ready to share, thus storing up treasure
for themselves as a good foundation for the future,
so that they may take hold of that which is truly life.
1 TIMOTHY 6:18-19 ESV

Dear Father, am I rich in good works? Am I generous and ready to share? I want to be. Sometimes, though, I get caught up in my own little world, in my own thoughts, and I don't notice the needs of others. How can I be generous if I don't pay attention to the needs around me? How can I share if I don't know where there's a lack? And how can I do good works that benefit others if I'm absorbed in myself? Open my eyes today, Lord. Show me where my gifts are needed. Show me where I can be useful and generous. I want to serve You and love others. Amen.

Hard Work

Go to the ant, O sluggard; consider her ways, and be wise. Without having any chief, officer, or ruler, she prepares her bread in summer and gathers her food in harvest.
PROVERBS 6:6–8 ESV

Dear Father, I want to teach my children a good work ethic. I want them to work hard and do things the right way, even when no one is looking. I know the way to do that isn't through lectures and platitudes. It's through living out, by example, what it means to work hard. It's by allowing them to have responsibilities and not doing things for them, even when it's easier to do it myself. Help me to work hard, even when I don't have a deadline or a supervisor. If I'm diligent with my work, I know my children will be, too. I know they will imitate me; teach me to imitate You. Amen.

What Is Good

He has shown you, O man, what is good; And what does the LORD require of you but to do justly, to love mercy, and to walk humbly with your God?
MICAH 6:8 NKJV

Dear Father, You truly have shown me in Your Word what is good. You want me to be like You. You are just, therefore You want me to be just. You want me to put aside any prejudice and view all people fairly. You are also merciful, showing us favor even though we don't deserve it. You withhold Your anger, even when I've done something to make You angry. Teach me to deal with others mercifully. Finally, You want me to walk humbly before You. That means I understand that You are God and I am not. Help me to be all these things, Father. I want to live out Your goodness every day. Amen.

All Talk

They profess to know God, but they deny him by their works. They are detestable, disobedient, unfit for any good work.
Titus 1:16 ESV

Dear Father, how many times have I denied You with my actions? I hope never, but I know there have been times when, though I say I love You, I don't act like I do.

How can I really love You when I say unkind things about Your children? How can I love You if I do things that displease You and hope no one finds out? If I tell the world I'm a Christian, yet my actions don't reflect Your character, I know that's detestable to You. Lord, I want my actions to make You proud to call me Your daughter. I confess my sins. I don't want to act that way anymore. Help me to show Your goodness to the world, not only through my words, but also through my actions. Amen.

On Things Above

*Set your minds on things that are above,
not on things that are on earth.*
COLOSSIANS 3:2 ESV

Dear Father, help me to set my mind on things above. I know when I'm thinking about You and Your goodness, my actions will naturally reflect Your love. But when I'm thinking about earthly things, such as how I'm going to pay the bills or how I'm going to get the laundry done or who said something that upset me, I get pulled down. When I think about those earthly things in light of Your goodness, though, I get lifted up. I know I can talk to You about anything in my life. The problem comes when I try to tackle those issues on my own without You. Remind me to set my mind on You as I come to You with every situation I face. May everything I do reflect Your love. Amen.

Quickly Obey

*I hasten and do not delay to
keep your commandments.*
PSALM 119:60 ESV

Dear Father, I've taught my children that delayed obedience is disobedience. I want them to obey me quickly. Yet, I sometimes delay my obedience to You because Your commands don't always fit with my desires. But I don't want to delay my obedience to You, Lord. I want to be quick to keep Your commandments no matter what. When I'm faced with a difficult decision, I don't want to even consider doing the wrong thing. I want my actions to always show my total commitment to You. Sometimes that may mean taking a moment to really consider what Your will is. It may mean taking time to pray, read Your Word, or seek wise counsel. I never want to delay action because I'd rather do the wrong thing. I never want to postpone obedience to You. Amen.

Special Gifts

*Since we have gifts that differ according to the grace
given to us, each of us is to exercise them accordingly:
if prophecy, according to the proportion of his faith;
if service, in his serving; or he who teaches, in his teaching.*
ROMANS 12:6–7 NASB

Dear Father, thank You for the gifts and talents You've given
me. Sometimes I compare my abilities to other people's and
feel like I'm lacking. But I know You created me with a purpose
in mind. Just as I see each of my children as unique and special,
I know that's how You view me. I don't want them comparing
themselves to others, so I shouldn't do it to myself. Help me
teach my children to use their special skills to glorify You and
help others. Give me opportunities to do the same as I pour out
everything I have for You. Amen.

Faith Comes by Hearing

*So faith comes from hearing,
and hearing through the
word of Christ.*
ROMANS 10:17 ESV

Dear Father, thank You for allowing me to live in a time and place where hearing Your Word is possible every single day. I can read Your Word any time I choose. I can turn on the radio or television and hear songs that praise You, or somebody talking about Your goodness. Yet I often allow my Bible to sit on the side table and gather dust. I make choices to watch shows that don't bring me closer to You. Father, I want to hear Your Word over and over. I want it to seep into my heart and into my children's hearts so our faith can grow. Remind me to read and listen to Your Word daily. Remind me to speak Your Word so my children can hear it. Help me to live in a way that will make my faith, and theirs, stronger. Amen.

I Believe

*And without faith it is impossible to please him,
for whoever would draw near to God must believe
that he exists and that he rewards those who seek him.*
HEBREWS 11:6 ESV

Dear Father, You told us in Your Word the definition of faith. In verse one of this chapter, it says faith is confidence in what we hope for, assurance of what we don't see. It is confidence and assurance in Your existence, Your love, and Your good plan for our lives. Do I exhibit that confidence in You, Lord? Or do I freak out at the first sign of trouble as if You don't exist? Forgive me for acting like I don't believe in You, Father. I know—with all that is in me, I know—You are loving and kind. You are working all things together for my benefit. I believe in You and in Your goodness. I have faith. Amen.

Like a Child

Trust in the Lord with all your heart, and do not lean on your own understanding. In all your ways acknowledge him, and he will make straight your paths.
PROVERBS 3:5–6 ESV

Dear Father, I'm learning more every single day what it means to trust You. Sometimes it's easy. . .like when everything's going smoothly. But other times it's really hard, Lord. At times my life seems to be falling apart, and I feel like I'm driving off a cliff with blinders on. In those times, it's hard to trust You, but I can learn much from my children. As infants they trusted me completely. They knew if they were hungry or scared or tired, they could come to Mommy, and I'd take care of them. They knew I would never hurt them. Help me to trust You that way, Father. I know I don't have to understand everything as long as I'm clinging to You. You will take care of me. Amen.

Where My Faith Rests

That your faith might not rest in the
wisdom of men but in the power of God.
1 CORINTHIANS 2:5 ESV

Dear Father, it sure would be nice if I could see You. If I could touch You, look into Your eyes, and hear Your audible voice, faith would be so much easier. But I guess that wouldn't really be faith, would it? Sometimes it's easier to go to my friends or some local or national expert with my problems. Their presence, along with their words of wisdom, soothes my spirit and gives me something tangible to hold on to. While it's always good to seek wise counsel, I know it would be foolish to listen to advice that goes against the wisdom found in Your Word. I have faith in Your power to act even when a situation seems impossible. When human logic contradicts the words found in Your book, I will choose Your wisdom. My faith rests in You alone. Amen.

Be Still

Be still, and know that I am God. I will be exalted
among the nations, I will be exalted in the earth!
PSALM 46:10 ESV

Dear Father, I'm not good at being still. Too many things
compete for my attention—every moment of every day, it seems.
Sometimes, it feels like the busyness of life is how I serve You
best, how I please You most. . .but that's not necessarily true.
Help me remember that I can become so wrapped up in doing
good things that I neglect the best thing, which is spending
quality time with You. Help me carve out a time and place to be
still, Father, and know You. When I spend time in Your presence,
it affects every area of my life. I'm able to love others better
when I've been with the source of love. Nudge my spirit to calm
down, relax, and simply bask in Your presence. Amen.

Faith Like Noah

*By faith Noah, being warned by God concerning
events as yet unseen, in reverent fear constructed
an ark for the saving of his household. By this he
condemned the world and became an heir of
the righteousness that comes by faith.*
HEBREWS 11:7 ESV

Dear Father, Noah had faith. In a place where it hadn't rained
in ages, he believed You. He heeded Your warning. You said it
would rain, and he knew You were true to Your word. You said
he'd need a boat, so he built one, despite his peers making fun
of him for it. Lord, help me have that kind of faith. You said it,
so I believe it. I want to be a boat-builder, or a person-builder,
or whatever kind of builder You want me to be. I believe Your
promises. I trust Your character. Give me faith like Noah. Amen.

Keeping the Faith

*I have fought the good fight, I have
finished the race, I have kept the faith.*
2 TIMOTHY 4:7 ESV

Dear Father, I haven't finished my race yet. I'm still running, still fighting the good fight. But I wonder—many years from now, when it's my turn to move from this life to the next—what will people say about me? Will they say I kept my faith in You, no matter what? I hope so. I'm sorry my faith wavers at times, depending on the circumstances. I know I can trust in You and Your goodness, no matter what may come. Yet when I forget who You are, I start clawing for control, and my faith disappears. Please forgive me. Help me to fight the good fight, finish the race, and keep the faith every day of my life. Amen.

Refuge and Strength

God is our refuge and strength, a very present help in trouble. Therefore we will not fear though the earth gives way, though the mountains be moved into the heart of the sea.

PSALM 46:1–2 ESV

Dear Father, life is hard and scary. Sometimes it feels like my world will tumble down around me. I don't like it when things don't go according to plan or when I can't control the outcome. It makes me feel helpless, and even hopeless. But with You, I always have hope. With You, there's always a safe place to go. You are my refuge, even when my life is crashing around me. You are my strength when I can't take another step. When everything goes as wrong as it can go, I'll run to You. I know You'll offer help and a safe place to fall. Remind me that I don't have to feel afraid as long as I trust in You. Amen.

He Will Hide Me

*For he will hide me in his shelter in the day
of trouble; he will conceal me under the cover
of his tent; he will lift me high upon a rock.*
PSALM 27:5 ESV

Dear Father, will You really hide me in Your shelter in the day
of trouble? Will You really conceal me? Sometimes it feels like
I'm being left to the wolves. Troubles growl from every side,
and trials threaten to eat me alive. But I know You are true to
Your Word. You promised to lift me high on a rock, out of reach
of those wolves. You promised to take care of me and keep me
from harm. When difficulties loom over my life, I will run to You.
I will wrap my arms around You and cling tight, knowing You
will protect me. I trust You. Remind me that I don't have to
feel afraid. Amen.

Trust in Him

Commit your way to the Lord; trust in him, and he
will act. He will bring forth your righteousness
as the light, and your justice as the noonday.
PSALM 37:5–6 ESV

Dear Father, I commit my way to You. Every step I take, everything I do, every word and every breath I dedicate to You. I want to please You, Father. I trust in Your love for me, and I know You have good plans for my life. Lord, I want Your righteousness to rule my life. The only way that can happen is if You cause it. My righteousness is nothing compared to Your holiness. Will You transform me? Will You make me like You? You also promised justice. Lord, You're aware of those areas where I've been treated unjustly. I know I don't have to think of revenge; You will bring about Your justice. Thank You for being such a kind, compassionate God. I trust You with my whole heart. Amen.

I Want You More

*But seek first the kingdom of God and his righteousness,
and all these things will be added to you.*
MATTHEW 6:33 ESV

Dear Father, I'm really good at looking for stuff. I shop around and find the best prices. I browse the Internet, reading reviews before I make a purchase. I'm even good at finding a lost shoe or the remote control. Every day it seems I'm seeking something. I also seek less tangible things, like friendship and love, peace and happiness. But I know, Lord, that everything I need can be found in You alone. When I seek You first, You fill me up. You give me peace and happiness. You are a friend like no other. You are the source of love. When I make You my primary goal, You bring blessings of every kind. No matter what I may want in my life, Lord, I want You more. You are my first priority. I love You. Amen.

Amazing Transformation

Do not be conformed to this world, but be transformed by the renewal of your mind, that by testing you may discern what is the will of God, what is good and acceptable and perfect.
ROMANS 12:2 ESV

Dear Father, so much of my life seems to be about conforming to the expectations placed on me. I need to act a certain way, look a certain way, participate in certain events. . .and while these things may not be bad in and of themselves, I don't want to become so caught up in conforming that I lose sight of what's important: becoming who You created me to be. I know if I let You, You'll transform me from my current state—a sinful, flawed human being—into someone who looks and acts very much like You. You'll take my temper and replace it with patience. You'll take my weaknesses and replace them with strengths. Lord, I want You to orchestrate an amazing transformation in my life beginning today. Amen.

No Other Gods

You shall have no other gods before me.
EXODUS 20:3 ESV

Dear Father, I would never put another god before You. Would I? When I think of gods, I often think of the little carved idols that were common in biblical times. But a god is really anything I serve and work for and pursue over You. A god is anything I think about more than You, anything I give a higher priority than my relationship with You. When I think of it that way, I have been guilty of putting You behind some other things in my life. I'm so sorry for chasing money or things or even relationships with other people more than I pursue You. Please forgive me, and remind me each day that no matter how important some of these things may seem, nothing is more important than You. I love You. Amen.

Managing My Household

For if someone does not know how to manage his own household, how will he care for God's church?
1 TIMOTHY 3:5 ESV

Dear Father, I feel like my life is a constant juggle of priorities. My children, my home, my job, my marriage, my volunteer responsibilities. . .not to mention myself. Every once in a while, I need a little *me* time. How do I know which of these things are important and which aren't? I know the most important task You've given me right now is to love those closest to me—my family. No matter how many good, worthy opportunities may compete for my time, I know I need to scale back until my main job is fulfilled: taking care of those who depend on me most. Years from now, few will remember who passed out flyers or baked a cake for the bake sale, but if my family feels neglected, that will have long-lasting consequences. Help me manage my household, Lord. Amen.

Keep My Commandments

If you love me, you will keep my commandments.
JOHN 14:15 ESV

Dear Father, I want to keep Your commandments. More than anything, I want to please You. It's easy to keep some of them. Others, though, are more difficult. I can say I love You with all my heart, soul, and mind. But when it comes to loving my neighbor. . .well, it depends on which neighbor. I know not to commit murder, but I wonder how many times I've killed a person's spirit with my words. I know not to commit adultery, but I have certainly envied what other people have. I know all Your commandments are centered around love: loving You and loving other people. Teach me to love more, to love better, as I learn to keep Your commandments. I love You with my whole heart, and I want my life to be a mirror of Your love for everyone to see. Amen.

Pursue Righteousness

Whoever pursues righteousness and unfailing love will find life, righteousness, and honor.
PROVERBS 21:21 NLT

Dear Father, I want to find life—real, abundant life—the way You promised. I want Your righteousness to be displayed in me, and I want honor, not for myself, but for You. You said many times in Your Word that if we seek You, we will find You when we seek You with all our hearts. The same is true for righteousness. We'll find it when we seek it. When we pursue unfailing love, we'll discover it. I know those things are key to abundant life, and they can only be found in You. In everything I do today, Lord, help me to pursue Your righteousness and Your unfailing love, pouring it out to others. I want to be a safe place for others as they experience Your holiness and peace displayed in my life. Amen.

Before Me

*I have set the LORD continually before me;
because He is at my right hand,
I will not be shaken.*
PSALM 16:8 NASB

Dear Father, I become easily distracted. I guess that's why I have to continually set You before me. Every day I get sidetracked by little chores that pop up, or I get caught up in a daydream or memory of some kind. If I'm not careful, those distractions can lead me down a slippery slope, and before I know it I'm embedded in worry about the future or anxiety about the past. Thank You for Your Holy Spirit and Your whispered reminders about where my focus should be. When I stay my mind on You, when I focus on Your will, when I cling to Your hand, I know I don't have to be afraid. Nothing can permanently hurt me as long as You are near. Amen.

Serving the King

Jesus said, "My kingdom is not of this world. If it were, my servants would fight to prevent my arrest by the Jewish leaders. But now my kingdom is from another place."
JOHN 18:36 NIV

Dear Father, I get preoccupied with my "earthly kingdom," but Your kingdom is the only one that matters. Your opinion is the only one that counts. You are my king, and I am Your servant. I am here to do Your bidding, which is to share Your love in any and every way I can with the people You've placed in my life. That service starts with my family as I pour words of life and encouragement into them. It continues as I do the same for others around me. When I build others up with Your love, I build Your kingdom. Remind me today to which kingdom I belong. Amen.

Doing His Will

*Then Jesus explained: "My nourishment
comes from doing the will of God, who sent me,
and from finishing his work."*
JOHN 4:34 NLT

Dear Father, sometimes I get depleted. I need some *me* time—
a day of shopping, a manicure, or even coffee with friends. I
know it's not wrong to nourish my spirit with things that bring
me joy. But Father, I want to be like Jesus. I want to draw
nourishment from doing Your will. I want to find such fulfillment
in serving others that I gain sustenance from it. I already serve
others, Lord, so the problem isn't in finding ways to perform
Your tasks. The issue is in my mind and attitude. Change my
heart, Lord, so that working for You and laying down my life for
others fills me up and makes me smile all the way down to my
toes. Like Christ, I want my nourishment to come from doing
Your will. Amen.

Time Alone

*But Jesus Himself would often
slip away to the wilderness and pray.*
LUKE 5:16 NASB

Dear Father, Jesus was Your Son. He was perfect, without sin, and one with You in every way. Yet even He needed to spend time alone with You. He had to sneak away and find solitude, just like I do. Help me find a time and place, Lord. Some little corner of some closet even, with a chair, my Bible, and a cup of coffee—time alone with You. If I need to wake up earlier or do something differently, show me how to carve out time to be still. I want to talk to You and listen to You. I need that time, Lord. And when You make time available, help me use it wisely and not get distracted with other things that won't fuel my spirit the way You will. And thank You, Lord, for wanting to spend time alone with me. Amen.

Two Are Better

Two are better than one, because they have a
good return for their labor: if either of them falls
down, one can help the other up. But pity anyone
who falls and has no one to help them up.
ECCLESIASTES 4:9–10 NIV

Dear Father, sometimes I want to go through life like the Lone Ranger. It's easier to go it alone; relationships are hard. But You want me to cultivate friendships with people in my family as well as outside my family. Help me to work and play well with others. Teach me to pay attention to others' needs, to encourage them, and to help them when I can. Help me to carve out time for relationships, Lord, even if it's just time for a cup of coffee or tea. I know You didn't make us to be alone. Help me be a good friend, a good coworker, a good wife, mother, daughter, and sister. I know the key to good relationships is love, so teach me to love. Amen.

Wounds from a Friend

Better is open rebuke than hidden love. Wounds from a friend can be trusted, but an enemy multiplies kisses.
PROVERBS 27:5–6 NIV

Dear Father, I don't like it when friends tell me things I don't want to hear. It's easy to become resistant, put up a wall, and go find someone who will parrot my opinions. But Lord, give me wisdom and humility. Help me recognize those people who truly care about me. If friends who have proven their love for me try to talk to me about something I'm doing wrong, or something that may harm my family or me, help me to listen. Even if I don't follow the advice, help me to truly, humbly consider it, knowing my friends only want the best for me. And when people who haven't proven their love tell me what I want to hear, help me take it with a grain of salt. All of this requires wisdom. Please give me wisdom in my relationships, Father. Amen.

What Friends Are For

*A friend loves at all times, and a
brother is born for a time of adversity.*
PROVERBS 17:17 NIV

Dear Father, I love this reminder that siblings are born to help
us throughout our lives when times are hard. But sometimes,
families don't work that way. Siblings don't always stick together
during adversity. That's why it's so important to develop lifelong
friendships. Help me to be the kind of friend and sibling today
that will foster that kind of love and commitment. Teach me to
feed those relationships during the easy times and to nurture
them during the difficult times. I know the way to have the
support I need during the hardship is to offer that support to
others when they need it, and to always build the bonds by
staying connected when times are good. Teach me to be a
good friend and to love at all times. Amen.

Love Like His

My command is this:
Love each other as I have loved you.
JOHN 15:12 NIV

Dear Father, You aren't simply the definition of love. You *are* love. If I want love to give to others, I must receive it first from You. You want us to love each other as You have loved us. You've been patient with me, so I should be patient with others. You've shown kindness to me, so I should be kind. You're generous and forgiving. You see the best in me and forget about the worst as soon as I apologize. You don't obsess over my flaws, but focus on my strengths. You are gentle. You aren't jealous when I receive something good; instead, You rejoice with me. You are always faithful, always honest, and always looking for ways to make me smile. Thank You for loving me, Father. Help me to love others the way You love. Amen.

The Company I Keep

Do not be deceived:
"Bad company ruins good morals."
1 CORINTHIANS 15:33 ESV

Dear Father, thank You for the reminder that bad company ruins good character. I know I should show love to all people, but I should use extreme caution when choosing the people I allow to influence my life. Often, I consider "bad company" to be the real, flesh-and-blood people I befriend. But truly, if I spend time with someone every day, I'll be influenced by their values. If I watch a television show every day, or read a blog, or hang out with the people on social media, I'll eventually succumb to their morals. Help me to guard my mind so I'm not swayed by views that oppose Your ways. Help me to surround myself with godly people and fill my mind with worthy views. Keep me pure, Lord. Allow me to be the influencer in my world as I share Your love in every way I can. Amen.

Choosing Teammates

*Don't team up with those who are unbelievers.
How can righteousness be a partner with wickedness?
How can light live with darkness? What harmony can
there be between Christ and the devil? How can a
believer be a partner with an unbeliever?*
2 Corinthians 6:14–15 NLT

Dear Father, in some ways, this verse seems to conflict with Your desire for me to share Your love with people who don't know You. How can I share You with someone if I don't have a relationship with them? Then again, You didn't say not to associate with unbelievers. You said not to team up with them. You said not to go into a partnership with them. I know this wisdom will serve me well. Even if someone seems upright at first—if they don't know You—our values will eventually clash. Give me wisdom about how to love people who don't know You without allowing them too much influence in my life. Amen.

Questions About Friendship

*The heartfelt counsel of a friend is as sweet as perfume
and incense. Never abandon a friend—either yours or
your father's. When disaster strikes, you won't have to
ask your brother for assistance. It's better to go to a
neighbor than to a brother who lives far away.*
PROVERBS 27:9-10 NLT

Dear Father, how am I doing when it comes to building and
maintaining friendships? I know it's important to have friends.
In Your wisdom, You made us for relationships, for You knew
we'd need each other. Do I have someone to talk to when I need
advice? Do I have a person I know I can count on in disaster?
If not, why? What can I do to keep my friendships strong? I
know that in order to have friends, I must be a friend. Forgive
me if I've neglected a friend or written off an offer of friendship
because I didn't have time. Teach me to be a loyal confidante
and companion to others. Amen.

About Forgiveness

For if you forgive others their trespasses,
your heavenly Father will also forgive you,
but if you do not forgive others their trespasses,
neither will your Father forgive your trespasses.
MATTHEW 6:14–15 ESV

Dear Father, thank You for forgiving me each time I mess up. As long as I say I'm sorry, You wipe it away. It's hard for me, sometimes, to forgive others. When someone offends me, I want to nurse my wound and hold a grudge. But that hurts me more than it does the other person. Give me grace to forgive, Father, and wisdom to know what that looks like. I understand I can forgive a person—and restore a right relationship with a Christian brother or sister—yet still set boundaries so they don't continue to hurt me. Teach me to forgive and to set proper guidelines in my relationships so that I'm protected from getting hurt again. Amen.

Serve One Another

For you were called to freedom, brothers.
Only do not use your freedom as an opportunity
for the flesh, but through love serve one another.
GALATIANS 5:13 ESV

Dear Father, thank You for the freedom I have in Christ. I don't have to follow a strict set of rules I know I'll never live up to. I honor You, not with rules, but with a heart that wants to serve You and serve others. Show me what service looks like, Father. Teach me how I can do things for others with a joyful heart. Help me to find strength and fulfillment in helping others who need my help. Give me the ability to see the difference between helping someone in need and helping someone who should be helping himself. In either case, give me grace, and let Your love pour out of my life. Allow me to see others through Your eyes as I live a life of love and service for You. Amen.

Stirring Things Up

*And let us consider one another in
order to stir up love and good works.*
HEBREWS 10:24 NKJV

Dear Father, what a fun idea! Thank You for this reminder to
study each other and look for ways to stir up love and good
works. It makes me laugh deep inside just thinking about it.
I picture a stealthy detective sneaking around, looking for ways
to make others smile, looking for chances to help them or make
them feel loved. I want to make that a way of life, Father. Help
me to keenly observe the people You've placed in my path and
identify opportunities to splash them with bits of Your love,
kindness, gentleness, and compassion. Who knows? Maybe
my actions will spur someone else to do the same for another
person and start a chain reaction of love and good works that
will make a real difference in this world. Help me stir things up
today, Lord. Amen.

SERENITY IN MY WORDS

What's Acceptable?

Let the words of my mouth and the meditation
of my heart be acceptable in your sight,
O LORD, my rock and my redeemer.
PSALM 19:14 ESV

Dear Father, I do things all the time for You. I clean house, do laundry, take care of church and civic duties. . .all of these, I do for You. Yet I know none of these things impress You. What You want from me is loving words and a pure heart. If I volunteer at church but grumble about it the whole time, You're not pleased. If I take care of my home and my children, yet I speak harshly to the people in my family, that's simply not acceptable. And if I spend hours on a project for You, but gossip about one of Your children, I risk hurting other people and making You angry. Let my words and thoughts be pleasing to You, Lord. Amen.

The Construction Business

*Do not let any unwholesome talk come out of your mouths,
but only what is helpful for building others up according
to their needs, that it may benefit those who listen.*
EPHESIANS 4:29 NIV

Dear Father, if words were money, I'd probably be more careful about how I spent them. I teach my children not to waste money on junk; help me learn not to waste my words on unwholesome talk. That could be foul language or angry words, gossip or slander, or even a conversation about something that's not pleasing to You. When it comes to my conversations, I want to be in the construction business, not the demolition business. Help me to build others up, not tear them down. I know my words can make a difference in people's lives, Father. Let my dialogue benefit all who listen and may it point them to You. Amen.

Wise Words

There is one who speaks rashly like the thrusts of a sword, but the tongue of the wise brings healing.
PROVERBS 12:18 NASB

Dear Father, I've known people who speak rashly, whose words slash and slice and cut through the spirit of some unsuspecting victim. I've even been the victim of those people at times. But Lord, I truly regret that I've been that person at times. I've not always been careful with my words, and I've let hurtful things slip through my lips. I'm so sorry, Lord. Please forgive me and heal anyone I've hurt with my words. I want others to crave my presence, not cringe from it. I want to be a safe place, not a scary prospect. I want my dialogue to point people to Your love. Give me wisdom and understanding. Let every word that comes out of my mouth bring healing and hope to those who listen. Amen.

Be Careful

---

*But I tell you that every careless word that
people speak, they shall give an accounting
for it in the day of judgment.*
MATTHEW 12:36 NASB

Dear Father, sometimes I can be so careless with what I say! I
speak without thinking, and before I know it, I've hurt someone's
feelings or made them angry, or I've stirred up a hornets' nest
of misunderstanding that takes a long time to make right. Why
can't I just stop and think before I let those words tumble out
of my mouth? I need help in this area, Lord. Give me wisdom,
patience, strength, and understanding. Help me to process my
speech in my head before I speak it out loud. Remind me to ask
myself if those words will bring hope and healing or if they'll
cause pain and misunderstanding. Help me to be careful with
my speech, Lord, so I can share Your love with those around me.
Amen.

Deadly Weapon

*Death and life are in the power of the tongue,
and those who love it will eat its fruit.*
PROVERBS 18:21 NASB

Dear Father, in the news I hear about all sorts of deadly weapons. Guns, knives, bombs, and cannons do great damage and cause immeasurable pain, but I don't think any of those are the deadliest weapons. Those things may kill the physical body, but that's nothing compared to the damage caused when we kill someone's spirit. How many times have my words pierced like arrows or shot like a cannon through someone's gut? I don't want to be a spirit-killer, Lord. I want my words to bring life. Help me to edit my dialogue before it exits my mouth. When I'm tired and cranky, or even when someone's words are hurting me, give me strength and discipline over my speech. I want every word I speak to bring healing and hope. Amen.

Staying Pure

But now you must also rid yourselves of all such things as these: anger, rage, malice, slander, and filthy language from your lips.
COLOSSIANS 3:8 NIV

Dear Father, I try to keep my heart clean. I try to keep my life pure. But no matter how hard I try, impurities seep in. I get frustrated and angry. I think catty, mean thoughts, and those thoughts often turn into words. Before I know it, my heart becomes smelly and putrid like stagnant water sitting in a bucket. But Lord, if that bucket sits under a flow of fresh water, the stagnant stuff will wash away. As long as it stays under the running spout, it will continue to be filled with pure, life-giving water. The same is true for my heart—if I want it to stay pure, I must remain in the flow of Your life-giving spirit. I must continue to fill my mind with Your words and continue to spend time in prayer. Keep my heart pure, Father. Amen.

Be on Guard

*Those who guard their mouths and their
tongues keep themselves from calamity.*
PROVERBS 21:23 NIV

Dear Father, how many times have I gotten myself in deep
trouble simply because I failed to control my tongue? *Too many.*
Thoughts pop into my head, and I let them slip out before I
really consider the consequences. Or worse, I don't even care
about the consequences, because I'm so angry I just want to
spew. When that happens, there's often a hefty price to pay. I
hurt others, and I hurt myself. Give me wisdom, Father, and help
me use it. Teach me to guard my mouth and rein in my words
before they cause damage to others and myself. Help me to
think carefully before I speak. Let my words build others up and
encourage them toward You. I want my speech to give life and
love to those around me. Amen.

Tight Rein

Those who consider themselves religious and yet do not keep a tight rein on their tongues deceive themselves, and their religion is worthless.

JAMES 1:26 NIV

Dear Father, some people consider me religious. I don't know if *religious* is the correct term, though. I'm just grateful to have a relationship with You. But regardless of the word used to describe it, others are watching me because they know I belong to You. They listen to my speech, and with every word, they're drawing conclusions about You. I know my children are watching and listening as well. When I speak of Your love, and then gossip about my friend or lose patience and say something harsh, or when I lose my temper and let a foul word slip, I send the wrong message about You. Forgive me for failing to control my tongue, Lord. Teach me better control, so all my words can present an accurate picture of Your love. Amen.

A Soothing Tongue

A soothing tongue is a tree of life,
but a perverse tongue crushes the spirit.
PROVERBS 15:4 NIV

Dear Father, I remember once when I was very sick, a friend brought me some hot soup, and the warmth soothed my throat. It didn't heal me immediately or fix all my problems, but it felt so nice. It was a comfort to my raw throat. I want my words to be like that. People around me have hurts that only You can heal. Yet my words can comfort them. My words can offer a soft refuge to their war-torn spirits. Keep me from speaking rashly and causing more pain to an already-sick soul. I don't want to crush anyone's spirit, Father. Instead, I want to be a tree of life, a healing balm to those You've placed in my path. Direct my speech, Father, and let my words be soothing today. Amen.

Seasoned with Salt

Let your conversation be always full of grace, seasoned with salt, so that you may know how to answer everyone.
COLOSSIANS 4:6 NIV

Dear Father, I love the word *grace*. It refers to the good things given to those who don't deserve them. You are full of grace toward me, and You want my words to be full of grace toward others. That means even if they've made me angry or if they're driving me crazy and pushing my patience to the limit, You want me to speak soft, soothing words of kindness and compassion. You want my words to offer life and hope. Just as salt takes a bland dish and makes it taste better, You want my words to make any conversation more pleasing. When I'm thinking this way—when my speech reflects Your love—it won't be nearly as hard to figure out what to say in any situation. I know I always need to answer with Your love. Give me grace in my speech today, Father. Amen.

Great Treasure

Behold, children are a heritage from the LORD,
the fruit of the womb a reward. Like arrows in the
hand of a warrior are the children of one's youth.
Blessed is the man who fills his quiver with them!
PSALM 127:3–4 NKJV

Dear Father, thank You for my children. I am so blessed to have them in my life; they are my treasures. Help me to cherish them, guard them, admire them, and take care of them the way I would any treasure, for they hold more value than many precious gemstones. Sometimes I forget to be thankful, Lord, for the breathtaking gift You gave me in them. Help me to love them, nurture them, and help them grow in You as they find their purpose here. Remind me to treat them gently, love them purely, and guide them with kindness and compassion. Thank You, Father, for my children. Amen.

That It May Go Well

Children, obey your parents in the Lord, for this is right. "Honor your father and mother"—this is the first commandment with a promise—"that it may go well with you and that you may enjoy long life on the earth."
EPHESIANS 6:1–3 NIV

Dear Father, thank You for Your promises, which lead us down the path toward the most peaceful life possible. Help me to teach Your principles to my children, for I want them to know Your blessings. When my children disobey, remind me to discipline them gently but firmly. When I require them to obey me, I set them up for success and for a life that goes well. When I require them to honor me, I set them up for a long, prosperous life. Remind me to hold high expectations but also to forgive them and disciple them when they fall short. Parenting is a hard job, Father. Thank You for guiding me on this journey. Amen.

Train Up a Child

Train up a child in the way he should go;
even when he is old he will not depart from it.
PROVERBS 22:6 ESV

Dear Father, thank You for this promise. It doesn't say my child will never push the limits or act out in rebellion. It does promise, however, that if I teach Your ways and model them, if I disciple my child consistently with love and compassion, Your ways will become an anchor in his life. When he tries to pull away, that training will pull him back to You. These early years are so important to my child's future, Father. Help me to be diligent in training with love and kindness as I plant seeds that will root and grow for the rest of his life. Remind me to model Your ways for him so he'll have a reference for godly living. Amen.

Diligent to Discipline

Whoever spares the rod hates his son,
but he who loves him is diligent to discipline him.
PROVERBS 13:24 ESV

Dear Father, it hurts me to discipline my children. I love them and don't like it when they're angry with me. When they say they're sorry, I just want to hold them and tell them it's okay. Sometimes it's easier just to give them a short lecture and avoid the drama and hassle of a consequence. But I know it's through early discipline that my children will develop good character. When I let them get away with disrespect or disobedience, I send the message that those things are okay. When they're older, they'll still think it's not a big deal to disobey or show disrespect. Help me be diligent in disciplining my children with appropriate consequences, all while showing kindness and compassion. I know this is one way I show them that I love them. Amen.

Left to Himself

The rod and reproof give wisdom, but a child left to himself brings shame to his mother.
PROVERBS 29:15 ESV

Dear Father, there are so many gadgets available today that will babysit my children for me. It's easy just to plug in a DVD or hand them an iPad and let them entertain themselves while I take care of business like housework or other chores. But Father, when I do that, it's easy to lose track of time. Before I know it, my children have been left to themselves for hours. My house may be clean . . . but at what expense? Help me to view those hours with a vision for the future. How much training—how much relationship building—could happen during that time? What memories am I forfeiting just to have a few moments of downtime? Holy Spirit, prick my heart when I'm in danger of leaving my children to themselves. Help me to be a wise parent who rears wise children. Amen.

Do Not Provoke

Fathers, do not provoke your children,
lest they become discouraged.
COLOSSIANS 3:21 ESV

Dear Father, sometimes my children drive me crazy! I tell them the same things over and over, yet it's like they've never heard it before. At times, I want to test them just to see if they'll remember what I've taught them. But Lord, if I offer those kinds of tests out of anger and frustration, I'm no better than a bully. If I yell and use sarcasm and try to get them to mess up, I'm provoking them. Why would I do that? But I do. I'm not proud of it, but sometimes when I've had a bad day, I provoke them without realizing what I'm doing. Give me a calm serenity, Lord. Let my every word and every action be lived out in love and gentleness as I model the patience You show me every day. Amen.

Setting the Example

In everything set them an example by doing what is good. In your teaching show integrity, seriousness and soundness of speech that cannot be condemned.
TITUS 2:7–8 NIV

Dear Father, am I setting a good example for my children in everything I do? That's a tough question. I know their little eyes, ears, and minds are like sponges absorbing my every word and deed. I know they want to be just like me; that's the way You designed it. When I teach them to act one way, and I act a different way, they'll learn more from my actions than my words. If I tell them to say only kind things, and they hear me gossiping or slandering another person, they'll grow to be gossips and slanderers themselves. Remind me each moment, Lord, that I have an audience. Help me to imitate You, so that when they imitate me, they'll be like You. Amen.

Including You

*And these words that I command you today shall
be on your heart. You shall teach them diligently to
your children, and shall talk of them when you sit
in your house, and when you walk by the way,
and when you lie down, and when you rise.*
DEUTERONOMY 6:6–7 ESV

Dear Father, help me make conversations about You a natural
part of our lives. Rather than relying on the preacher or the
Sunday school teacher to take care of my children's spiritual
training, I need to include You in our family's daily tasks. When
we see a beautiful flower, remind me to thank You for it out loud
so my children can hear. When we're preparing dinner, remind
me to mention Your precept that if we don't work, we shouldn't
eat. By making Your Word a casual part of our conversations,
I teach my children that You are to be honored every day, every
moment. . .not just on Sundays. Remind me, Lord, to include
You. Amen.

Because They're Mine

My son, do not make light of the Lord's discipline,
and do not lose heart when he rebukes you,
because the Lord disciplines the one he loves,
and he chastens everyone he accepts as a son.
HEBREWS 12:5–6 NIV

Dear Father, I don't like it when You discipline me. But even though it's not pleasant, Your discipline makes me feel safe and reminds me that I belong to You. If You didn't care about me, You'd leave me alone and let me do whatever I wanted. Because I'm Your child, You take the time to teach me and correct me when I'm wrong. In the same way, I know I need to discipline my children. It's not always pleasant, but I do so because I love them and want what's best for them. Help me to discipline with love and consistency. I know my discipline helps my children feel safe and gives them a sense of belonging. Amen.

Teaching Reverence

From everlasting to everlasting the Lord's love is with those who fear him, and his righteousness with their children's children.
Psalm 103:17 niv

Dear Father, thank You for promising Your love to me and to my children. I know that by living my life with respect and reverence for Your Word and Your laws, I can bring blessings on my life and the lives of my children and grandchildren. Lord, I want to model godly, righteous living for my children. I want to teach them what it means to fear You: not a cowardly fear, but an awed reverence. I know the way I treat them will influence the way they feel about You as they learn to honor and respect me. Help me, Lord. I know the more I honor You, the better parent I'll be. I love You. Amen.

Covenant of Peace

*"Though the mountains be shaken and the hills be removed, yet my unfailing love for you will not be shaken nor my covenant of peace be removed," says the L*ORD*, who has compassion on you.*
ISAIAH 54:10 NIV

Dear Father, wow. What a beautiful, comforting promise. No matter what comes, whether it's earthquakes, tornadoes, cancer, divorce, or unemployment, no matter what . . . Your love will never fail me. It will never leave me. Not only that, but Your peace will go with me wherever my journey leads. Through the lowest ravine, over the highest mountain, and everywhere in between, Your peace will follow me. You love me, and You have compassion on me. No matter what may come, I know I don't have to go looking for Your peace. It's already right there. Thank You for Your peace, Father. Amen.

Led Forth in Peace

*You will go out in joy and be led forth in peace;
the mountains and hills will burst into song before you,
and all the trees of the field will clap their hands.*
ISAIAH 55:12 NIV

Dear Father, thank You for this beautiful promise. Though troubles may come and block my path, I'll get through them with Your help. You will lead me over each bump with a big dose of Your peace. And once I come through them, You promise joy! I will come out on the other side of any conflict with beautiful music and trees waving their branches for me. What a lovely, poetic reminder of Your promise to lead me forth in peace and of Your promise of abundant inner happiness and contentment. Anxiety can be a thing of the past as I trust in You and Your goodness. Thank You for Your promises and Your peace. Amen.

Come to Me

Come to me, all you who are weary and burdened,
and I will give you rest. Take my yoke upon you and
learn from me, for I am gentle and humble in heart,
and you will find rest for your souls. For my yoke
is easy and my burden is light.
MATTHEW 11:28–30 NIV

Dear Father, some days I feel so tired. I'm so glad You invite the weary and burdened to come to You for rest. You even invite us to take Your load, which is easy and light. Lord, You said to learn from You, and I'd find rest for my soul. What do I need to learn? I'm a ready and willing learner. You said You are gentle and humble in heart. . .perhaps that's what I need to learn—to be gentle and humble. Somehow, those qualities will help me find serenity and rest. Teach me, Father. Make me like You. Amen.

The Peace Giver

Peace I leave with you; my peace I give you.
I do not give to you as the world gives. Do not
let your hearts be troubled and do not be afraid.
JOHN 14:27 NIV

Dear Father, when Christ left this earth to return to heaven, He promised to leave peace with us. He promised to continue giving peace through the Holy Spirit. When the world gives me peace, it's temporary. I can have an hour of peace at a spa or perhaps a few hours at the beach. Then real life will return, and the chaos will continue. But the kind of peace You give remains through the chaos, through the storms and trials. Your peace is a quiet place within, where we know You are. It's a place our spirits can cuddle in Your arms and rest. I know as long as I have You, I don't need to fear any storm. Thank You, Father, for Your peace. Amen.

Make Every Effort

Let us therefore make every effort to do what leads to peace and mutual edification.
ROMANS 14:19 NIV

Dear Father, one of the greatest causes of stress in my life is relationships gone sour. People say or do things, or don't say or do things, and feelings get hurt. And to be honest, some people are just harder to get along with than others. But I'm not telling You anything You don't already know, am I? Please help me make a commitment to get along with everyone, no matter what. If that means swallowing my pride and biting my tongue, so be it. If that means encouraging someone who's not exactly my favorite person, help me do it. I know at times I'm not the easiest person to deal with either, but You still show me patience. Help me make every effort to show a loving, gracious, peaceful attitude toward everyone. Amen.

Consistent Peace

For God is not a God of disorder but of peace—
as in all the congregations of the Lord's people.
1 CORINTHIANS 14:33 NIV

Dear Father, sometimes my life is pretty disorderly. With too many commitments and too many people depending on me, things don't always fall into place the way I want them to. I know You will help me maintain order in my life. But Father, the most important place I need to show order and consistency is in my own heart and attitude. Even if the house is a mess, I want my children to know Mom is always the same: loving, patient, gentle. Even if my schedule is interrupted, I want my response to stress to show a consistent serenity. The real chaos comes when I am erratic in my moods—calm one moment, freaked out the next. Help me to maintain order in my spirit. You are unchanging in Your nature. Help me to be unchanging in love, patience, kindness, compassion, and peace. Amen.

Free Gifts

May the God of hope fill you with all joy and peace
as you trust in him, so that you may overflow
with hope by the power of the Holy Spirit.
ROMANS 15:13 NIV

Dear Father, I want to overflow with hope. I want to feel confidence in the prospect of good things to come. I know Your Holy Spirit gives me that hope; it's already there. . .I just have to claim it. When I take hold of that hope, when I look at the future and smile, knowing good things are waiting, I also get a couple of bonus gifts: joy and peace. It makes me smile to know You want me to feel joy. You want to delight me with thrilling gifts. You also want me to have peace, and You've already provided it. It's as close as Your Holy Spirit who lives inside me. Help me to embrace Your hope, Your joy, and Your peace today, Father. I trust in Your goodness. Amen.

Following the Map

*Those who love Your law have great peace,
and nothing causes them to stumble.*
PSALM 119:165 NASB

Dear Father, I love Your law and Your ways. I love Your written Word that teaches me how to live. The more I study Your ways, the more I love them. Father, I want to become addicted to Your law, for I know it holds the keys to a fulfilling, abundant life. Within Your Book, I find guidance for relationships, finances, work ethic, and everything else I might encounter. Though our lives here on earth will never be perfect, I know that by making the choices to live the way You want me to, I will increase my chances for a life of peace and fulfillment. The more I follow You, the less chance I have to really mess things up. Thank You for providing me with a roadmap for peaceful living. Help me to follow it. Amen.

I'm Listening

*I will hear what God the Lord will say;
for He will speak peace to His people, to His
godly ones; but let them not turn back to folly.*
Psalm 85:8 NASB

Dear Father, help me to be a good listener. I get so easily distracted, and I don't always hear Your whispered words. But if I listen carefully, I hear peace. Even in the midst of chaos, Your voice is there, sighing peace into my spirit. When I get distracted, I tend to pay attention to things that will only cause me grief. I guess those distractions cause me to turn back to folly like the verse says. I don't want to do that; how foolish I am to ever listen to any voice but Yours! Though the world screams around me, though temptations roar and trials rumble, help me drown out those noises. Even when I must lean forward to hear You, I know Your voice is there. Speak peace to me, Lord. I'm listening. Amen.

Overcomer

"These things I have spoken to you, so that in Me you may have peace. In the world you have tribulation, but take courage; I have overcome the world."
JOHN 16:33 NASB

Dear Father, You know that tribulation thing You spoke of? You weren't kidding. I long for a time and place when everything is as it should be. No more problems with relationships or finances. No more health issues. No more struggle or pain or bitter tears. But in spite of these things, I know I can find peace in Your promises. I know I can walk through each day and through any circumstance with my head high, a smile on my face, and a song in my heart, for I have hope. I know my future is filled with good things both in this life and in eternity. Let my life be a reflection of that hope to those around me as I walk in the serenity of Your love. Amen.

Scripture Index